TAO TE CHING:

AN INSIGHTFUL AND MODERN TRANSLATION BY J. H. MCDONALD

ANNOTATED &
ILLUSTRATED BY
BOBUI ROSUI &
JOE PROMEDIO

LAO TZU

FRONTISPIECE: Panda Pooch Witnessing A Passing of the Torch (Bobu Rosu, 2024)

art of zentrification

www.artofzentrification.ca
attains nirvana summer 2024

TAO TE CHING:

AN INSIGHTFUL AND MODERN TRANSLATION BY J. H. MCDONALD

Explore the Wisdom of the Tao. A Beautifully
Illustrated Edition of the Enigmatic Lao Tzu's
Masterpiece Tao Te Ching

ANNOTATED &
ILLUSTRATED BY
BOBUIROSU &
JOE PROMEDIO

LAO TZU

art of zentrification

PHILOSOPHICAL BRANDALISM

manufacturing meditative states since 2018
manufacturing meditative states for others since 2023

digitally integrated coloring & activity books, children's books
jigsaw puzzles, apparel, and more!

YOUTUBE　　　INSTAGRAM　　　FACEBOOK　　　AMAZON

IN MEMORIAM DOCTORUM
(in memory of great teachers)

"we are ready for the next quantum leap in human consciousness."

PAUL STAMETS

TAO TE CHING:

AN INSIGHTFUL AND MODERN TRANSLATION BY J. H. MCDONALD

PART 1: ANNOTATIONS

PART 2

TAO TE CHING

EGALITARIAN HISTORY X

Taoism finds its roots in the mists of prehistoric China, emerging from the depths of contemplation and observation of the natural world, At its heart lies the concept of the Tao—the Way—the fundamental essence underlying all existence. Picture the Tao as the flowing river, ever-changing, yet eternal; it is the rhythm of the cosmos, the harmony of opposites, the ineffable essence of being.

Legend whispers tales of a sage named Lao Tzu, whose wisdom is enshrined in the sacred text, the Tao Te Ching. This enigmatic tome, a beacon of insight and paradox, guides seekers along the path of effortless action, urging them to embrace the spontaneous flow of life and harmonize with the Tao.

Through the centuries, Taoism intertwined with the rich tapestry of Chinese culture, influencing art, poetry, medicine, and martial arts. Its teachings seeped into the hearts of emperors and peasants alike, offering solace in times of turmoil and guidance in moments of clarity.

The yin and yang, symbolizing the complementary forces of the universe, dance across the pages of Taoist thought, reminding us of the delicate balance between light and shadow, action and non-action, existence and non-existence.

As the centuries unfurled, Taoism evolved, giving rise to diverse schools of thought—from the philosophical musings of Chuang Tzu to the mystical practices of alchemy and inner cultivation.

Yet, amidst the ebb and flow of history, the essence of Taoism remains timeless—a gentle whisper in the wind, inviting us to surrender to the flow of the Tao, to embrace the simplicity of being, and to find harmony in the eternal dance of existence.

THE THREE WISE GUYS

CONFUCIUS   **LAO TZU**   **CHUANG TZU**

It is hard to give context to a book that is two and a half thousand years old, but we still have to try. As we delve into the lives and teachings of three luminaries whose wisdom continues to illuminate the path of enlightenment: Confucius, Lao Tzu, and Chuang Tzu, and notice the interplay between them, one will find the verses of this book unravel themselves a little easier. It helps us engage in what I call 'exercises in empathy', helping us to see an object or event from multiple perspectives, as well as objectively. It is not about agreeing, it is about understanding. Comfort is the enemy of progress.

Born in the tumultuous era of ancient China, Confucius dedicated his life to the cultivation of ethical conduct and righteous governance. His teachings, as preserved in the Analects, emphasize the importance of filial piety, social order, and the pursuit of self-improvement as the foundations of a harmonious society.

Lao Tzu, the enigmatic sage whose words echo through the annals of time. Emerging from the misty realms of ancient China, Lao Tzu expounded upon the ineffable essence of the Tao—the Way—the guiding principle underlying all existence. In the Tao Te Ching, he extolled the virtues of simplicity, spontaneity, and non-action, urging seekers to harmonize with the natural rhythms of the universe.

Finally, we encounter Chuang Tzu, the master of paradox and existential inquiry. With his whimsical anecdotes and profound reflections, Chuang Tzu invites us to transcend the limitations of conventional thought and embrace the boundless expanse of the Tao. Through tales of transformation and metamorphosis, he illuminates the fluidity of existence and the illusory nature of the self.

Though each sage followed a unique path and espoused distinct teachings, they shared a common thread—their deep reverence for the Tao. Confucius sought to cultivate moral character and social harmony, Lao Tzu advocated for simplicity and spontaneity, while Chuang Tzu delved into the mysteries of existence and the nature of reality. Yet, amidst their differences, they all recognized the interconnectedness of all things and the profound wisdom inherent in the eternal dance of the Tao.

In the golden age of ancient China, amidst the swirling currents of change and tradition, there emerged a sage whose teachings would shape the moral fabric of a nation—Confucius.

Born in the state of Lu in 551 BCE, Confucius, known as Kong Qiu in his native tongue, came into the world during a time of political upheaval and social unrest. Despite the turmoil of the era, he grew to become a beacon of wisdom and virtue, leaving an indelible mark on the hearts and minds of generations to come.

From an early age, Confucius exhibited a thirst for knowledge and a profound sense of moral duty. He delved deep into the ancient texts of Chinese tradition, seeking to understand the principles of righteousness, filial piety, and social harmony.

Confucius's journey of enlightenment led him to serve in various governmental roles, where he sought to implement his vision of ethical governance and societal order. Yet, frustrated by the corruption and injustice he encountered, he embarked on a quest to impart his teachings to future generations, believing that true change begins with the cultivation of moral character.

It was during this period of exile and introspection that Confucius compiled his seminal work, the Analects—a collection of dialogues, aphorisms, and teachings that encapsulate his vision of a harmonious society governed by virtue and benevolence.

In the Analects, Confucius emphasized the importance of self-cultivation, filial piety, and the cultivation of moral character as the foundations of a just and prosperous society. His teachings, characterized by their practical wisdom and ethical rigor, resonated deeply with scholars, rulers, and commoners alike, shaping the moral consciousness of East Asia for centuries to come.

Though Confucius passed from this world in 479 BCE, his legacy endures— a testament to the enduring power of moral virtue and the timeless wisdom of the sage. From the halls of academia to the corridors of power, his teachings continue to inspire seekers of truth and righteousness, guiding them along the path of self-improvement and social harmony.

Born in the 6th century BCE, the exact details of Lao Tzu's life are shrouded in myth and legend, blending seamlessly with the enigmatic essence of his teachings. Some say he was born in the province of Henan, others claim he hailed from the state of Chu. Yet, amidst the ambiguity, one thing remains clear: his wisdom transcends the confines of history, resonating with seekers across the ages.

Lao Tzu's path led him to serve as a keeper of the archives in the imperial court of Zhou, where his keen intellect and profound insights captivated the hearts of rulers and scholars alike. Legend has it that disheartened by the corruption and chaos of court life, he embarked on a journey to the western frontier, seeking solace in the embrace of the timeless Tao.

It was during this fateful journey that Lao Tzu encountered the keeper of the Jade Gate, who, recognising the sage's boundless wisdom, implored him to share his teachings before departing into the wilderness. And so, in a moment of divine inspiration, Lao Tzu penned the timeless wisdom of the Tao Te Ching, a testament to the ineffable essence of the Tao—the Way—the guiding principle of existence itself.

In the Tao Te Ching, Lao Tzu expounded upon the virtues of humility, simplicity, and harmony, urging seekers to embrace the spontaneous flow of life and find peace in the midst of chaos. His words, imbued with poetic grace and philosophical depth, continue to inspire generations of truth-seekers, guiding them along the path of enlightenment and self-realisation.

Though the details of his life may fade into obscurity, the legacy of Lao Tzu endures—a beacon of light in a world shrouded in darkness, a reminder of the eternal wisdom that resides within us all.

Born in the fourth century BCE, Chuang Tzu, also known as Zhuangzi, hailed from the state of Meng, in what is now modern-day Anhui province. Little is known of his early life, but his legacy as one of the greatest philosophers of Taoism is woven into the fabric of Chinese thought.

Unlike his contemporary Confucius, who sought to elucidate the path of social harmony and ethical conduct, Chuang Tzu delved into the realm of metaphysics and existential inquiry. He wandered the countryside, engaging in dialogues with scholars and sages, challenging conventional wisdom and unravelling the mysteries of existence.

Chuang Tzu's teachings, preserved in the eponymous text, the Zhuangzi, are a tapestry of allegory, paradox, and philosophical insight. Through whimsical anecdotes and profound reflections, he invites readers to transcend the limitations of conventional thought and embrace the boundless expanse of the Tao—the Way—the underlying principle of all existence.

Central to Chuang Tzu's philosophy is the concept of "ziran," or natural spontaneity—the idea that true freedom arises from aligning with the natural course of events, rather than resisting or controlling them. He extolled the virtues of wu-wei, or non-action, advocating for a life of effortless flow and harmonious engagement with the world.

Yet, amidst the profundity of his philosophical musings, Chuang Tzu infused his teachings with a playful spirit and a keen sense of humour. He regaled his disciples with tales of transformation and metamorphosis, illustrating the fluidity of existence and the illusory nature of the self.

Though Chuang Tzu's life may fade into the mists of time, his legacy as a pioneer of philosophical thought endures—a testament to the enduring quest for truth and enlightenment. From the tranquil groves of ancient China to the bustling cities of the modern world, his words continue to inspire seekers of wisdom, inviting them to dance with the ever-changing rhythms of the Tao.

In the boundless expanse of wisdom literature, few texts shimmer with the enigmatic allure of the Tao Te Ching. Its verses, like whispers from the eternal cosmos, transcend time and space, guiding seekers on a journey of profound self-discovery and spiritual awakening. To delve into its pages is to embark upon an odyssey of the soul, navigating the depths of existence with grace and serenity.

Legend shrouds the origins of this ancient masterpiece, attributing its authorship to the sage Lao Tzu. Once a topic of debate, it is now widely accepted that the man who put a little punk rock into the religious punch is likely to have never existed. Written some time around the 6th century BCE, it is one of the oldest texts in Chinese literature. Nonetheless, its wisdom is timeless despite its age.

Composed of 81 short chapters, each verse flows with poetic language, colorful imagery, and is rich with philosophical insight. The Tao Te Ching's brevity and ambiguity allow for multiple interpretations. I return to it with such frequency that the copy I purchased five years ago has never even made it to my bookshelf.

At the heart of the philosophy lies the concept of the "Tao"—the natural order of the universe, the underlying principle that governs everything—a concept that has profoundly influenced Chinese philosophy and culture.

Another fundamental concept echoing through the verses is "Wu Wei," or "non-action," which emphasizes acting in accordance with the Tao, without force or struggle. The Tao Te Ching also introduces the complementary forces of Yin and Yang, reflecting the dualistic nature of existence.

Despite its ancient origins, the Tao Te Ching remains relevant today, inspiring philosophers, scholars, and spiritual practitioners worldwide, and is still one of the most widely translated texts our species has ever produced.

In this illustrated edition, we are honored to present the Tao Te Ching alongside the masterful artwork of Bobu Rosu, whose journey mirrors the essence of the Tao itself. Bobu's nomadic existence and profound insights into Zen Buddhism, its roots in Taoism, and the punk rock ethos he adopted from his bandmates playing bass for Tibetan hardcore pioneers 'Buddhist Priest', make his departure from Japan remarkably similar to Lao Tzu's legendary disappearance into the mountains past the northwestern border of China.

Through Bobu's lens, the Tao Te Ching is rendered accessible to modern audiences, its ancient wisdom distilled into a form easily digestible for today's generation. As we journey through its pages, accompanied by Bobu's artistry and insights, may we find solace and inspiration in the timeless wisdom of the Tao. And though Bobu's physical presence may elude us, his spirit lives on in these pages, guiding us on our quest for truth and understanding.

JP

HENRY DAVID THOREAU FROM COVER ART SUPPLIED BY BOBU FOR AN ART OF ZENTRIFICATION PUBLICATION OF 'CIVIL DISOBEDIENCE'. SCAN THE CODE THE LISTEN TO 'CIVIL DISOBEDIENCE' READ BY JOHN VEGGIE ON THE ART OF ZENTRIFICATION YOUTUBE CHANNEL.

Born in Hokkaido, Japan, on August 9, 1945, at precisely 11:02 am, Bobu's arrival bore witness to the tumultuous birth pains of a new era. His dear mother freed the nearly thirteen-and-a-half-pound Bobu after a three-day endurance trial of intense labor. Her water had broken shortly after the Little Boy arrived in Hiroshima, and as the Big Boy arrived in Hokkaido, there was a Fat Man falling from the sky over Nagasaki.

KUMIKO & BOBU ROSU, 8/14/45
(FIVE DAYS AFTER BOBU WAS BORN)

Kumiko's struggle mirrored the resilience of the human spirit amidst the chaos of war as her mother Yukio watched on. She was delighted by the sights and sounds of the young girls pain. Yukio did not approve. Not only was Kumiko unmarried, but the girl had also not yet told her apathetic life giver who the father was. Her own father Yaz hung his head in shame, trying to hide the occasional tear that streamed down his face from his oppressive wife.

Kojiro Kobayashi, The infants father, was a member of the Japanese Navy aboard the I-41 submarine when it was sunk by American warships and aircraft. The submarine's crew, including Bobu's father, perished on November 18, 1944, seventeen days after Bobu was conceived. His bones were among the many scattered across the pacific ocean floor by the strong currents that flowed along them. Many have been assimilated by reefs as far away as Manila, where hundreds of seasoned divers visit a skull embedded in a calcified section of reef to watch clown fish dance in and out of its cavity through its eye sockets.

Kumiko was not in love with Kojiro. They were school friends. She had felt sorry for him, as many girls her age did as they watched boys being called men only for the purposes of war. Kojiro was scared. So many of the boys his age were, and for due cause. He would almost certainly die without knowing much of what life had to offer. Kumiko could offer only one thing, love beyond that of his mother's. Despite her sympathy, she did not take pity on Kojiro. She did it because Kojiro needed courage. It mattered not if it was misplaced. She did not expect to see him again.

BOBU 3/17/47

Kumiko's mother was in such stark opposition to the war that she feared that if she knew the boy was an officer, regardless of his willingness to be there, Bobu would be taken far away and put up for adoption. She worried that she may never see him again. Kumiko could not allow this. Even if she could not raise the boy herself, she had to be near him.

Kumiko, brave and strong, took the contractions in silence for the first 24 hours. After 48, the discomfort could be seen on her face. In the 60th hour, Kumiko was now in agonizing pain. In between deep breaths, vulgar obscenities directed toward her mother flowed like unobstructed chi. By hour 65 she could no longer bear the pain. She gave the name, not of the true father, but a patsy. An unusual one, but as it goes, Kumiko was not a dumb girl.

the man she claimed was the boys father was Eiko Zenji. Eiko was the Roshi at nearby Engakuji temple. After the words escaped her lips between deep, but weakening breathes, she used what little energy she had left to demand something to relieve her pain, and gave her mother one last thing to think about

『この哀れな獣よ、最後の月経が長江のように流れますように』

She met eyes with her fathers. He could not hide the smirk on his face her words had caused. She collapsed on the bed and entered the home stretch of her marathon.

BOBU AND HIS BELOVED DALI, A GIFT HE RECIEVED ON HIS SECOND BIRTHDAY FROM ROSHI EIKO ZENJI, ENGAKUJI TEMPLE 8/8/47

Three weeks after his birth Bobu would be taken to the Engakuji temple by Kumiko's mother and father, a decision that left Yaz bitter and resentful. He had grown to detest his wife and could no longer look at her face. When they arrived they were greeted by one of the students. Yukio hissed Zenji's name at the him and without a word he quickly disappeared in search of the infamous Roshi.

EIKO ZENJI

Zenji appeared smiling, bowing first to Yukio, then Yaz, then Yukio once more. Yukio, known for her rudeness, hastily returned the bow before she began to scold the man for his perversions, and the beast he created. He stood motionless, his eyes steadfast in their kindness, beaming at the boy with a wide smile that revealed his well-kept, naturally imperfect teeth.

The Roshi bowed and thanked the pair, saying nothing as he reached to take Bobu from Yaz's trembling arms. Feeling the resistance in Yaz's grip, Zenji paused and looked deep into Yaz's eyes. They were not the eyes of Yaz the man. Eiko was looking into the eyes of Yaz the child. In their reflection, he could see Yuki, the puppy Yaz had received as a gift for his tenth birthday. Moving slightly to cast more light on the reflection, he could see the dog's lifeless young body after it had been struck by a passing kidō densha (軌道電車). Yaz was broken, confused, scared. His eyes, too upset to cry, quivered noisily in their sockets. It was the first time Yaz would experience death. The guilt he felt that afternoon would never leave him. When Zenji's compassionate gaze met Yaz's, the rattling of his quivering eyes faded as his eyes filled with tears. Yaz felt all of the Roshi's love and compassion in his heart but it would not be enough. Yaz would experience his second death firsthand two short weeks later when he would end his own life.

PHOTOGRAPHING SAKURA
BLOSSOMS 5/22/1951

Yaz, a highly revered engineer working for the recently founded Toyota, devised an elaborate plan to frame Yukio for his murder. Despite maintaining her innocence throughout her trial, she would be convicted and sentenced to serve the remainder of her life in the women's wing of Abashiri Prison where she would meet her untimely death.

After news of her crimes had reached the prison, it was not long before members of the Shugo Tenshi (守護天使) prison gang were planning Yukio's demise. The Shugo Tenshi were a ruthless gang of Yakuza women who targeted new inmates whose crimes involved the harming of a child in any way. Yukio Rosu, in the minds of the Shugo Tenshi, was a new kind of monster, one that would be dealt with accordingly.

YAZ & YUKI (1930) BY EMIKO NAKAMURA
WATERCOLOR ON CANVAS

ENIKO NAKAMURA, A CELEBRATED KYOTO-BORN PAINTER WAS YAZ'S MATERNAL GRANDMOTHER. IN AN INTERVIEW SHORTLY BEFORE HER DEATH SHE SAID THAT SHE HAD MADE PLANS TO DESTROY THE PAINTING BUT COULDN'T BRING HERSELF TO DO SO, SAYING "THERE IS SO MUCH DARKNESS IN THAT BOYS HEART, THIS WAS THE LAST TIME I EVER SAW HIM SMILE." THE PAINTING IS A PART OF THE EMINAK EXHIBIT AT THE KYOTO MUSEUM OF ART.

Eiko Zenji slowly walked towards the couple, gently bouncing baby Bobu in his arms. Bobu was fascinated by the man's contrastingly bald head as Eiko's steps slowly edged the pair backwards toward the exit, giving them time to reconsider. But, as steadfast as Zenji was in his kindness, Yukio was in her wickedness. When the couple were far enough outside the monastery door, he looked directly into the eyes of Yaz with his warm, loving gaze and nodded. His gaze then shifted to Yukio, as he sharply pointed his tongue at the woman before lifting one of his bare feet and gently pushing the door closed.

One week later, as the sun was going down, Kumiko was on the monastery doorstep seeking shelter. When the door opened, she was met by Eiko Zenji.

"Ahh," he smiled, "you're just in time. He is getting hungry."

Bobu was said to be remarkably mature in his spiritual development at a young age. Some believed the boy would fulfil a prophecy, and he would be called by some "the bomb to end all bombs," by others "the retaliatory strike". He would however embark on a spiritual journey that would defy convention. Rising swiftly through the ranks of the Rinzai school at the Engakuji Temple, he was poised to attain the highest honor, Roshi, before he chose a different path.

Disillusioned with the trappings of tradition, he excommunicated himself, embracing self-imposed exile and a nomadic existence travelling the world in search of an expanded teaching of the Buddha. On the morning of April 8, 1974, secured to the temple door by a Hello Kitty thumbtack, a note was left by Bobu. It was found by Kumiko shortly after dawn flapping against the wooden entrance like a koi removed from its pond. Bobu had left Japan. Devastated, she shared the news with the temple residents before retreating to her quarters where she swore to never speak until Bobu's return.

This silence did not end until thirty-six years later when Kumiko received an unmarked package. Inside it was an iPod Touch, and instructions on how to use this thing called "FaceTime". When she finally figured out how to turn the device on she found in its contacts a teddy bear icon, beside it Bobu's name. They have sat together from thousands of miles away every Sunday at 9pm (Tokyo time) to watch The Simpsons.

BOBU, MORNING MEDITATION, 6/25/57

菩薩が地理的に仏教発祥の地でのみ生まれ変わらなければならないと考えるのは単純だろう。さまざまな土地に、さまざまな姿、さまざまな肌の仏陀がたくさんいました。それらを見る先見の明も、それらを解放する洞察力も持たない意志によって統治される土地。ここの学生たちは私を必要としません。彼らは、かろうじてさまよう心を落ち着かせる公案とともに、快適な経典の中に安全に身を寄せているからです。だから私は今、カンフーのケインのように地球を歩くためにあなたを残します。場所から場所へと歩き、人々に会い、冒険に出かけましょう。仏陀が私を望んでいる場所に連れて行ってくれるまで、私は歩きます。永遠にかかるなら、私は永遠に歩きます。私はただのボブであり、それ以上でもそれ以下でもありません。私は新しい学校を始めるつもりですが、それは古い学校に根ざしたものになります。就学前の人は言うことができます。壁も経典もない世界。それはカナワギの波のように広大な陸地を横切り、生徒たちの目を欺く幻想を洗い流します。
コーエン禅師の言葉を贈ります。

「久しぶりのマリアンヌ、
始める時が来ました
笑う、
そして泣きます、
そして泣きます、
そして笑う
それについてはもう一度。」

さよなら愚痴
ボブ

 TO OPEN BOBU'S LETTER USE GOOGLE TRANSLATE
SET TO READ JAPANESE ON YOUR PHONE

When Bobu asked me to write the foreword for this book, I was taken aback. Me? I retold to him his own stories, I pointed out all the important people he had met, the artists he counted amongst his friends. Me. I'm just a guy.

"That is why it should be you. You found what everyone wants, what everyone is looking for, when you yourself weren't even looking."

I contest, "If I found it, then why am I still looking?"

Bobu smiles before gently speaking, "How do you know you're still looking for it and that you are not looking for them?"

I look at Bobu through puzzled eyes.

"The only thing better than being one with the Tao," he says, "is two being one with the Tao. Or three, or four."

Bobu & I 1987

BOBU & LEONARD COHEN IN LAS VEGAS AT BILL MURRAY'S WEDDING, SUPERBOWL SUNDAY 1981

I nod my head. "I'm picking up what you're putting down."

He casually reached into his left pocket while his right hand disappeared into the cloud of hair that bounced with his every step. As his hands returned to my field of vision, he reached out and said, "You are overthinking it, maybe this will help."

He passed me a small card, and about two and a half centimeters of a HB pencil that was about as sharp as Noam Chomsky's sense of humor.

"Don't you know Bono?" I asked, still trying to shake the assignment, "I bet he would love to write a foreword for you."

After a short pause, Bobu says to me sternly, "Fuck that guy, he still hasn't found what he's looking for."

After looking at each other for a moment in silence, we erupt in laughter.

Bobu has had possibly one of the most interesting lives ever lived. For fifty years he has been travelling west, chasing the sun. Seventy-six times he has circled the globe, once entirely on foot, except where it was not possible. Never taking the same road twice, he has always been where he needed to be when he needed to be there. If you Google Bobu, you are not likely to find much more than a sparse Wikipedia page. He left a trail of lectures and commencement speeches captured on audio or film reels in the vaults of prestigious art schools around the world. Like Lao Tzu, he is an enigma, but a search and rescue team has been dispatched in search of these reels to hopefully restore and remaster these nearly lost glimpses into the mind of a gentle genius into a single collection as the Bobu Rosu Artful Living Audio Archive.

When I was dispatched to tackle my assignment, he at least gave me a place to start. He gave me a telephone number where I could reach his mother. "Call her Okaasan," were his instructions.

I was nervous to call. There was no rational reason for it. She must be an angel, I thought. Only an angel could have brought someone like Bobu into the world.

I collected myself, took a deep breath, and began dialing.

It rang twice before I heard the receiver lift on the other end.

A gentle voice spoke, "Bobu bear?"

I froze. I didn't know how to begin.

"Konichwa?"

"Hello Okaasan... I am a friend of Bobu's..."

I heard something drop on the other end of the line.

"Bobu?" her voice cracks. The dryness in her throat screams the worry felt in her heart.

"No Okaasan, Bobu is just fine. I'm calling to talk to you."

"To me?!" she replied doubtfully. "What are you talking about Willis?"

Caught off guard, a single loud "ha," escaped me like a hiccup.

"I introduce myself, telling her that Bobu and I are working on a book together before I say, "Your son has had quite an extraordinary life, Okaasan, how much of what he tells me is true?"

She laughs before shifting personas, "The truth?! You can't handle the truth!" she yells on the other end.

"Bobu doesn't lie. If anything he downplays his adventures," she says. now Exorcised of Jack Nicholson's demon.

That's cute, I thought, a mother defending her seventy-eight-year-old child's honor.

"I used to know who the people were in the pictures he would send home. David Bowie, Nelson Mandela, The Beatles, Salvador Dali, Martin Luther King Jr, Bob Marley, Bruce Lee...so many." She pauses as she takes a sip of tea and continues, "Now I don't know who or what a Beastie Boy is, or a Wu-Tang Clan."

We exchange stories about ourselves before I pop the big question, "Okaasan, tell me; what was Bobu like as a boy?"

BOBU AND ADAM YAUCH (MCA) OF THE BEASTIE BOYS AT THE FIRST TIBETAN FREEDOM CONCERT, SAN FRANCISCO, USA 6/15/96

THE BOMB TO END ALL BOMBS (2018) STREET ART INSTALLATION BY ARTIST UNAGI MAKI AT THE KOENJI MURAL CITY PROJECT, TOKYO, JAPAN.

加藤聡

TOP (L-R) BOBU PORTRAIT, (SPRAY SPECTER GADGET, HARAJUKU
NEIGHBORHOOD) "MOAB" (KUMIKO ROSU BY SATOSHI KATO, SHIBUYA
DISTRICT) "SHAKE IT TIL YA BREAK IT" (RYOICHI YAMADA, TENNOZU ISLE)

BOBU ROSU IN KINGSTON JAMAICA FOR THE RECORDING OF HIS REGGAE ALBUM SNEAKY PETE & THE RACOUS REBELS 9/25/78

Our conversation lasted nearly five hours. It wasn't until I heard the bells on the other end of the line to signal morning meditation did time snap back into my reality structure. The bells were signaling that it was time for morning meditation. I had kept her up all night. Kumiko let out a long yawn and I began steering the conversation to its conclusion. I asked if there was anything else she could think of that might help me. She said that there was one more thing.

She said that shortly before Bobu's first birthday a letter arrived at the temple for her. Quickly retreating to her quarters, she put Bobu down for a nap, sat on her bed and opened the envelope.

"To my Miko," it began...

A YOUNG MAN GETS SERVED AT A NIGHT CLUB IN HARLEM. NEXT TO MEDITATION BREAK DANCING WAS BOBU'S FAVORITE ACTIVITY UNTIL A HERNIATED DISK FORCED HIM TO RETIRE FROM THE PASTIME PERMANENTLY.

It was a letter from her father. In it, Yaz explained to his daughter what had happened that fateful afternoon. He told her a story from when he was young, about a gift he received for his birthday, and the guilt he lived with each day since. How he couldn't shoulder the weight anymore. He asked for his daughter's forgiveness, told her that he loved Bobu with all his heart, and that he loved her too. He closed the letter with a lullaby he used to sing to her when she was a child.

月の子守歌

月明かり　やさしく
星たちも　微笑む
眠る君　夢の中
守るよ　僕らが

おやすみ　おやすみ
夜は長いけど
明日が来るまで
夢の中で会おう

風のささやき　そよぐ
木々のさえずり　きこえる
夜はまだ　続くけど
君を守るよ　僕らが

眠りの中で　冒険しよう
世界の果てまで　一緒に行こう
明日が来る前に　すべてが
夢の中で叶う

Her tiny frame quaked from her sobs as she read it. Out of the envelope, onto the floor fell a tiny photograph Kumiko had never seen before this moment. It was her and Yaz when she was an infant.

She told me that she had never told anyone this secret. This was for nothing but to protect her father from the shame associated with suicide. To let his soul rest in peace.

After a long pause, she said, "I expect to see this part included in your foreword."

Surprised, I asked why now the change of heart.

"Joe, my dear," she says, "the world is hurting deep down in its soul. We have grown tall, we have grown wide, and we have grown old. It is time now to grow up. Time to look at the hammer in our hand and ask ourselves, what are we doing? Are we creating, or are we destroying? Are we helping, or are we hurting? Are we giving, or are we taking? We should not care whether the choice to leave this world is right or wrong. We should care that the choice was made. We need to look deeply into the cause, not the morality of the effect. The Tao Te Ching has all the answers to living a fulfilling life. All but one. Suicide. I'm afraid that at the time of its writing, living was the prime objective."

I thanked her for her help, and for giving Bobu to the world. It was obvious wisdom ran deep in the family's genetics.

She giggled modestly, "What are you doing Sunday at 9 o'clock, Tokyo time? I just learned how to use Zoom."

There was a brief pause as I heard her shuffling through nearby papers. "This week's guest list includes Zach de la Rocha, Dennis McKenna, Talib Kweli, and Barack Obama. We have room for one more. We will be watching Bobu's favorite episode, the one where Lisa becomes a Buddhist."

I allowed for a few days to process everything Kumiko had told me and found I went from one problem to another. I needed material for a foreword, and got a story so rich it would take a trilogy of novels to do justice.

YAZ (AGE 10) WITH YUKI

BOBU (AGE 13) WITH MIHO.

YAZ AND MIKO 4/20/29

A - ANTHROPOCENTRISM: PLACING MAN AT THE CENTER, A VIEW THAT HAS SPARKED MUCH DEBATE ABOUT OUR PLACE IN THE COSMOS. B - BENEVOLENCE: A VIRTUE OF GOODWILL THAT FOSTERS HARMONY AMONG INDIVIDUALS. C - CONTEMPLATION: THE ACT OF DEEP REFLECTIVE THOUGHT, A CORNERSTONE OF PHILOSOPHY. D - DIALECTIC: A METHOD OF ARGUMENT AND INQUIRY, THROUGH WHICH TRUTH IS SOUGHT. E - EMPIRICISM: THE THEORY THAT ALL KNOWLEDGE IS DERIVED FROM SENSE-EXPERIENCE. F - FINITUDE: THE CONDITION OF HAVING LIMITS, WHICH SPURS US TO SEEK MEANING WITHIN OUR TEMPORAL BOUNDS. G - GRAVITAS: A QUALITY OF DEPTH IN CHARACTER, OFTEN SOUGHT IN PHILOSOPHICAL DISCOURSE AND CONDUCT. H - HUMANISM: A PERSPECTIVE THAT EMPHASIZES THE VALUE AND AGENCY OF HUMAN BEINGS. I - IDEALISM: THE BELIEF THAT REALITY IS MENTALLY CONSTRUCTED OR IMMATERIALLY MIND-DEPENDENT. J - JUSTICE: A FUNDAMENTAL VIRTUE, THE PURSUIT OF WHICH IS KEY TO A WELL-ORDERED SOCIETY. K - KNOWLEDGE: THE FOUNDATION OF PHILOSOPHICAL EXPLORATION AND THE QUEST FOR UNDERSTANDING. L - LOGOS: REASON OR THE PRINCIPLE THAT ORDERS THE COSMOS; THE SEARCH FOR IT UNDERPINS RATIONAL DISCOURSE. M - METAPHYSICS: THE BRANCH OF PHILOSOPHY CONCERNED WITH THE NATURE OF EXISTENCE AND REALITY. N - NIHILISM: THE REJECTION OF ALL RELIGIOUS AND MORAL PRINCIPLES, OFTEN IN THE BELIEF THAT LIFE IS MEANINGLESS. O - ONTOLOGY: THE PHILOSOPHICAL STUDY OF THE NATURE OF BEING, BECOMING, EXISTENCE, OR REALITY. P - PRAGMATISM: A PHILOSOPHICAL TRADITION FOCUSING ON THE PRACTICAL APPLICATION OF IDEAS AND THE TRUTH OF ACTIONS. Q - QUEST: THE PURSUIT OF PHILOSOPHICAL WISDOM, SIMILAR TO THE SOCRATIC JOURNEY FOR UNDERSTANDING. R - RATIONALISM: THE BELIEF THAT REASON IS THE CHIEF SOURCE OF KNOWLEDGE. S - SOCRATIC METHOD: THE TECHNIQUE OF QUESTIONING AND DIALOGUE TO STIMULATE CRITICAL THINKING AND ILLUMINATE IDEAS. T - TELEOLOGY: THE STUDY OF THE PURPOSES OR GOALS THAT PROCESSES OR ENTITIES SERVE. U - UTILITARIANISM: A MORAL THEORY THAT ADVOCATES ACTIONS THAT MAXIMIZE HAPPINESS AND WELL-BEING FOR ALL AFFECTED INDIVIDUALS. V - VIRTUE: THE EXCELLENCE OF CHARACTER, A CENTRAL THEME OF SOCRATIC TEACHINGS. W - WISDOM: THE INTEGRATION OF KNOWLEDGE, EXPERIENCE, AND DEEP UNDERSTANDING; THE ULTIMATE GOAL OF PHILOSOPHY. X - XENIA: THE ANCIENT GREEK CONCEPT OF HOSPITALITY, WHICH INCLUDES BOTH GUEST-FRIENDSHIP AND GENEROSITY. Y - YEARNING: THE HUMAN DESIRE FOR KNOWLEDGE AND TRUTH, A DRIVING FORCE IN PHILOSOPHICAL INQUIRY. Z - ZENTRIFICATION: THE ENHANCEMENT OF MENTAL AND SPIRITUAL QUALITIES, REFLECTING THE TRANSFORMATIVE AIM OF PHILOSOPHY.

BRING THE RUCKUS: BOBU'S LEGACY

Bobu Rosu, a troubadour of the modern epoch, weaves a mandala of tales not with silk and thread, but with the sinew of shared human experience. His character—much like a chalice—overflows with the wine of empathy and insight, drawing us into his narrative of communion and wisdom.

In the theatre of life, Rosu plays many parts: a sage draped in the humble garb of a poet, an observer whose eyes glint with the mischief of unspoken truths, and a wayfarer whose footsteps echo with the rhythms of ancient lore. His voice, a fulcrum balancing levity and profundity, carries the mirth of a storyteller well-versed in the art of life's tragic comedy.

Each chord struck by Rosu resonates within the caverns of the soul, compelling us to face the music of our own existence. He navigates the grand narrative with the deftness of a philosopher-king, drawing from the fount of Taoist harmony, Buddhist equanimity, and absurdist tenacity to construct a world view that gleams with the polish of considered thought.

In the presence of Bobu Rosu, one finds the unfolding of a character rich with contradictions: he is the whisper of wisdom in a cacophony of folly, the steady hand in the tremulous quiver of uncertainty, and the jest that cuts through solemnity's guise. His is a spirit carved by the hands of enlightenment thinkers yet unbound by the strictures of eras and ideologies.

Through his words and deeds, Rosu embodies the still point in our turning world, an axis of serene reflection amid the tumultuous sea of being. In him we find not just a character, but a beacon illuminating the path toward a deeper understanding of the selves we inhabit, and the shared journey we navigate beneath the vast tapestry of the cosmos.

I kept the card as a souvenir to remind me of the most unforgettably kind and radiant human being I have ever met. If given the opportunity to choose different i would have used the card to write a foreword in seven words, and handed it back to Bobu. A man with the grace of simplicity he possesses probably would have liked it more.

'Bobu Rosu ain't nothin' to fuck with'

I have since made copies of Bobu's card. I never leave home without at least one. If I encounter someone in the course of my day who I think could use it, I casually hand it to them in passing. Constantly moving to be far enough away when they are looking at it and scratching their head. I have included some copies on the final pages of this book.

As per Bobu's final request, I will conclude with my master thesis, which was more of a challenge really. Bobu always stresses that you don't truly know something until you can express it using different language and metaphors than through which it was learned. There were no parameters, expectations, or limitations. "Write something that tells me you understand," he said, "If you have to sharpen your pencil to write more, you don't understand."

Tough, but fair, and always consistent. That is why Bobu is the best teacher.

"NO WAY!" "WAY!"

A TAOIST REFLECTION
BY JOE PROMEDIO

IN THE BEGINNING, THERE WAS NOTHING
EXCEPT THE ETERNAL TAO.

ETERNITY WAS BORN AT ONCE, OF NOTHING AND EVERYTHING,
IT FLOWED EFFORTLESSLY, UNOPPOSED,
LIKE AN OUT-OF-BODY EXPERIENCE,
FROM THE SOURCE OF THE UNIVERSE,

EXPERIENCING ITSELF AS BOTH THE
OBSERVER AND THE OBSERVED.
OBSERVING THE UNIVERSE, AS THE UNIVERSE.
IMMACULATE CONCEPTION.

THEN WHAT OF FORM?

THE TAO IS THE SUN, THE MOON, THE STARS,
AND EVERYTHING IN BETWEEN.

EVERY RIVER FLOWS WITH THE TAO.
EVERY BRANCH OF EVERY TREE, SHAPED BY THE TAO.
EVERY ROOT HELD IN PLACE BY THE TAO.

EVERY GRAIN OF SAND, A GRAIN OF THE TAO.
EVERY BLADE OF GRASS, A BLADE OF THE TAO.
EVERY DROP OF RAIN, A DROP OF THE TAO.

EVERY CLOUD IS AN EXPRESSION OF THE SPIRITUAL TAO,
EVERY MOUNTAIN, AN IMPRESSION OF THE MATERIAL TAO.

THEN WHAT OF MEASURABLE TIME?

FAKE NEWS.

SPRING, SUMMER, FALL, WINTER, AND SPRING AGAIN...

THE RHYTHMS OF NATURE, NO MINUTE HAND,
NO TIMESTAMPS, NO ALARMS, NO SURPRISES.
FROM ONE LIFE TO THE NEXT, THAT IS THE TAO...
THE PASSING OF THE SEASONS. NO MORE. NO LESS.

WHO IS THE TAO?

THE TAO IS EVERYONE, YET IT IS NO ONE.
SHAPELESS, NAMELESS, ETERNAL.
THE TAO IS OF GOD, AS GOD IS OF MAN, AS MAN IS OF TAO.

THEN WHAT OF THE GODS?

THE GODS BORN FROM THE MINDS OF MEN HANG THEIR HEADS
IN THE PRESENCE OF THE TAO, THUS THEIR HEADS HANG
ALWAYS, EVERYWHERE, FOREVER, OVERENCUMBERED WITH
THE SHAME OF A COLD AND FATED ANCHOR.

FOR IN THE EYE'S OF DEITY'S THE TAO IS
MORE WEIGHTLESS THAN THE FEATHER OF AN ANGEL.
IT IS RASCALITY PERFECTED, OPEN-SOURCE, AND SCALABLE.

TO EMBRACE IMPERMANCE IS TO RELEASE PRECONCEPTION.
TO RELEASE PRECONCEPTION IS TO DEFY CONVENTION.
TO DEFY CONVENTION IS TO LOVE IMPERFCTION.

TO LOVE IMPERFECTION IS TO LEARN THE
WAY OF UNCONDITIONAL HAPPINESS THROUGH
A SONG FLOATING ON THE BREEZE,
WHISPERING A CHORUS FOR THOSE WHO CHOOSE TO HEAR IT;

"VICARIOSLY VULNERABLE, PRECARIOUSLY BEGUILED,
WITH THE UNFETTERED UNCONSCIOUS OF AN UNWARY CHILD.
IMPERCEIVABLY UNCONCEIVABLE. IMMEASURABLY UNBELIEVABLE.
UNIMAGINABLY BEAUTIFUL. UNQUANTIFIABLY ONE..
THIS IS THE TAO;

SIMPLICITY. HUMILITY. COMPASSION
FRICTION. EMBRACE. RESISTANCE. COEXISTENCE.
MEDITATION. PEACE...AND LOVE.
FOREVER AND EVER

ZAZEN.

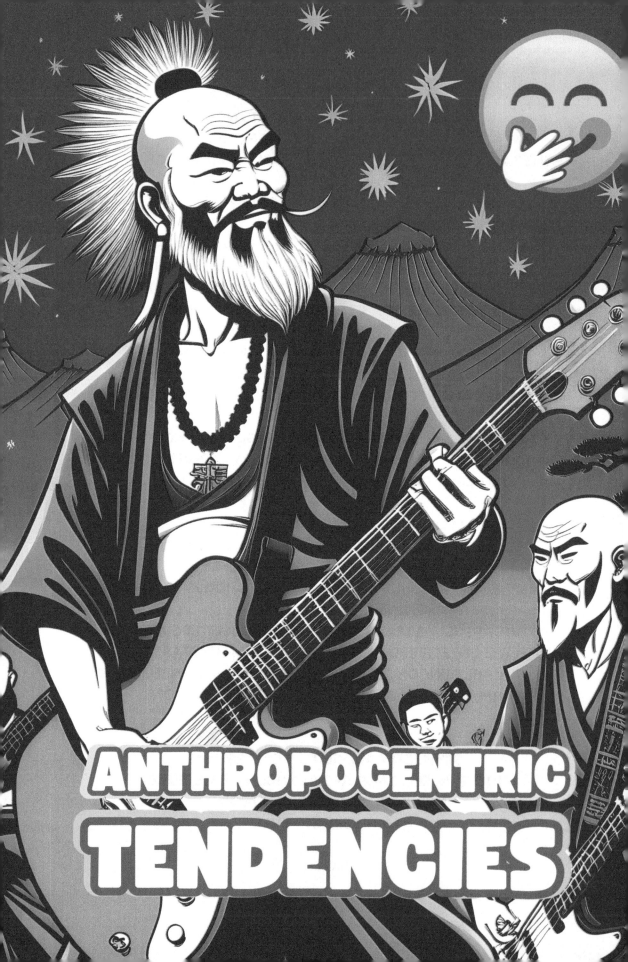

THE LAW OF HOLES
THE ZENTRIFICATION CONSTITUTION

The First Law of Holes:

"If you find yourself in one, stop digging."

Philosophically, the first law of holes resonates deeply with the Socratic maxim "know thyself." In Socratic philosophy, self-awareness is the cornerstone of wisdom and the starting point for genuine intellectual and moral progress. Socrates believed that acknowledging our own ignorance is the first step towards enlightenment.

The Second Law of Holes:

"When you stop digging, you are still in a hole."

The Second Law of Holes, "When you stop digging, you are still in a hole," carries profound philosophical implications, particularly resonating with existentialist principles that delve into the nature of responsibility, agency, and the imperative for proactive engagement in the face of challenges.

BOBU ON SET OF RETURN OF THE JEDI 1981.

The Third Law of Holes:

"A hole not filled will cause more issues in the future."

The Third Law of Holes, "A hole not filled will cause more issues in the future," unfolds a philosophical narrative that intertwines with ecological principles, sustainability ethics, and the profound insights of interconnectedness found in various philosophical traditions.

The Fourth Law of Holes:

"Don't jump in another person's hole."

The Fourth Law of Holes, "Don't jump in another person's hole," introduces a profound ethical dimension into the philosophical framework of the Law of Holes. This law navigates the delicate balance between compassion and individual autonomy, resonating with ethical considerations found in the philosophical principles of Immanuel Kant and shedding light on the complexities of altruism.

The Fifth Law of Holes:

"Put logic above your ego."

The Fifth Law of Holes, "Put logic above your ego," delves into the intricate interplay between rational decision-making and the often complicating factor of human ego. This law, grounded in cognitive-behavioral principles, carries profound philosophical implications by inviting individuals to prioritize rationality over the potentially obstructive influence of ego-driven decision-making.

These laws are an integral component of the Zentrificationism philosophy and will be discussed in detail in a book on the subject to be released in the not too distant future.

THE THREE TREASURES

天下皆謂我道大，似不肖。夫唯大，故似不肖。若肖久矣。其細也夫！我有三寶，持而保之。一曰慈，二曰儉，三曰不敢為天下先。慈故能勇；儉故能廣；不敢為天下先，故能成器長。今舍慈且勇；舍儉且廣；舍後且先；死矣！夫慈以戰則勝，以守則固。天將救之，以慈衛之。

LIN YUTANG,CHINESE LINGUIST, NOVELIST, AND PHILOSOPHER, SAID THAT CHAPTER 67 OF TAO TE CHING CONTAINED LAO TZU'S "MOST BEAUTIFUL TEACHINGS"

 VIEW THROUGH YOUR PHONE'S CAMERA **CHINESE**

In the tapestry of existence, there are three treasures, three precious jewels that shimmer amidst the fabric of our lives. These treasures, rooted deep within the essence of being, offer profound insights into the nature of existence and our place within it.

The first treasure is known as Jing, the treasure of essence. It is the vital force that flows through every atom, every cell, every being in the universe. Jing is the raw material of existence, the substance from which all things emerge. It is the silent pulse of life, the rhythm of creation and dissolution that weaves through the cosmos. To attune ourselves to Jing is to align with the primal energy of the universe, to recognize the inherent interconnectedness of all things.

The second treasure is Qi, the treasure of energy. Qi is the dynamic force that animates the universe, the invisible currents that surge through the fabric of reality. It is the breath of life, the vital energy that flows through our bodies, our minds, and our spirits. Like the ebb and flow of the tides, Qi moves in cycles of expansion and contraction, growth and decay. To cultivate Qi is to harness the power of life itself, to awaken to the boundless potential that resides within each moment.

The third treasure is Shen, the treasure of spirit. Shen is the radiant light of awareness that illuminates the darkness of ignorance. It is the pure essence of consciousness, the timeless presence that transcends the limitations of time and space. Shen is the eternal flame that burns within every heart, the source of wisdom, compassion, and love. To embody Shen is to realize the true nature of reality, to awaken to the infinite potentiality of the present moment. Together, these three treasures form the foundation of existence, the sacred trinity that guides us on our journey through life. To cherish Jing, Qi, and Shen is to honor the interconnectedness of all things, to recognize the inherent unity that binds us to the vast tapestry of the cosmos. In the embrace of these treasures, we find liberation from the illusions of separation and suffering, and discover the boundless joy of being alive.

IT IS TIME TO...

wake up to what is possible,
grow up and mend where we are broken,
and show up and do that which needs to be done.

It's worth taking a stand for basic decency. It may be the last thing you get to stand for. The only thing stopping us from reclaiming honor, courage, duty, sacrifice, and democracy, is us.

This is not about left/right, this is about fear or love. (btw, democracy isn't supposed to have wings. It is supposed to be a circle. That is how it keeps everyone inside when it's working.)

We should all ponder the question: "Is it possible for me to put aside my own ambitions momentarily to ascend to a higher vantage point? Can I scale the peak, survey the landscape, and acknowledge what must be done, irrespective of whether recognition comes my way? Whether my role is a mere footnote or a critical pivot, the point is that I must fulfill _my_ role" Should each of us undertake even the smallest acts of kindness—be it holding a door for someone burdened by their load or engaging in dialogue across ideological lines to affirm our shared values of love, beauty, and truth—we honor democracy and each other. The task is straightforward. It's about transcending deception to find solutions that accommodate diverse viewpoints.

these are the types of conclusions we must reach!

EIKO ZENJI

SEPTEMBER 16, 1908

-

APRIL 7, 1994

TAOISM: A PUNK-ISH PHILOSOPHY
HEY! HO! LET'S GO!

To the seekers of discord and harmony, the rebels of the system, and the silent wanderers of the Way: this foreword is an invocation, a challenge to the spirit that unites the thrashing chords of punk rock with the silent wisdom of Taoism. It is a call to those who find solace in the tumult and tranquility alike, to consider the profound kinship between these seemingly disparate realms. For within their cores resonates a shared heartbeat, a pulse of defiance against the superficial and the inauthentic, a battle cry for compassion in a world often marred by indifference.

Let this foreword unsettle you, as it is meant to provoke thought and stir the soul. The pages that follow will not offer the comfort of simple truths or the warmth of familiar rhetoric. Rather, they are an odyssey through the chaos and calm, a juxtaposition of brash punk anthems and the serene verses of Laozi, each a beacon guiding us towards a deeper understanding of self and society.

Punk rock, with its raw, visceral energy, is not the antithesis of Taoism's contemplative stillness but its unexpected companion. Both are radical expressions of life's essence—a life unfiltered and unfettered, a life that demands we confront our pretenses and strip bare the facades that divide us. They teach us that humility is not weakness, simplicity not poverty, and subversion not mere destruction, but rather, that these are the virtues upon which a more profound existence is built.

Do not be fooled by the surface-level noise of punk or the quiet depths of Taoism. To engage with either is to confront the visceral starkness of reality.

HEY! HO! LET'S GO!

Punk screams the truths we attempt to stifle, while Taoism whispers the wisdom we struggle to hear. Both demand of us a visceral engagement with the world—an engagement that is immediate, unpretentious, and unyieldingly authentic.

As you delve into the convergence of these two worlds, be prepared to dismantle your preconceptions. Allow the anarchic spirit of punk to shake the foundations of your convictions, just as the Taoist flow erodes the rigid structures of your beliefs. Herein lies the subtle art of subversion, not through mindless rebellion or passive acquiescence, but through the radical act of living with intention and integrity.

This text is a testament to the vibrancy of a life lived at the confluence of passion and peace, a life where empathy is the strongest currency, and understanding the ultimate pursuit. To those who dare to explore this union, who are ready to embrace the paradox and find unity within the dissonance: may you emerge with a deeper sense of kinship and a renewed vision for what it means to live authentically.

Let the provocation begin!

A NOTE ABOUT THE TRANSLATION USED

Rather than translate the Tao with Joe myself, I used a modern translation by John H. Macdonald. This translation was produced specifically for the public domain in 1996, making it a popular translation that is accessible to a modern generation.
I would like to add that along with its accessibility, the use of language is efficient, making it a pleasant text to return to time and time again. As is said, you will pick up something new with each run through the Tao. It seems no one knows much of this J.H. Macdonald which leads me to believe someone wished, as Lao Tzu did, to remain obscured from history.

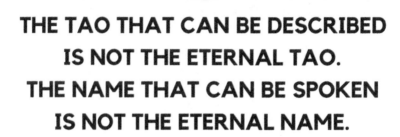

THE TAO THAT CAN BE DESCRIBED
IS NOT THE ETERNAL TAO.
THE NAME THAT CAN BE SPOKEN
IS NOT THE ETERNAL NAME.

THE NAMELESS IS THE BOUNDARY OF
HEAVEN AND EARTH.
THE NAMED IS THE MOTHER OF CREATION.

FREED FROM DESIRE,
YOU CAN SEE THE HIDDEN MYSTERY.
BY HAVING DESIRE,
YOU CAN ONLY SEE WHAT IS VISIBLY REAL.

YET MYSTERY AND REALITY
EMERGE FROM THE SAME SOURCE.
THIS SOURCE IS CALLED DARKNESS.

DARKNESS BORN FROM DARKNESS.
THE BEGINNING OF ALL UNDERSTANDING.

WHEN PEOPLE SEE THINGS AS BEAUTIFUL, UGLINESS IS CREATED.
WHEN PEOPLE SEE THINGS AS GOOD, EVIL IS CREATED.

BEING AND NON-BEING PRODUCE EACH OTHER.
DIFFICULT AND EASY COMPLEMENT EACH OTHER.
LONG AND SHORT DEFINE EACH OTHER.
HIGH AND LOW OPPOSE EACH OTHER.
FORE AND AFT FOLLOW EACH OTHER.

THEREFORE THE MASTER CAN ACT WITHOUT DOING ANYTHING
AND TEACH WITHOUT SAYING A WORD.
THINGS COME HER WAY AND SHE DOES NOT STOP THEM;
THINGS LEAVE AND SHE LETS THEM GO.
SHE HAS WITHOUT POSSESSING, AND ACTS WITHOUT ANY EXPECTATIONS.
WHEN HER WORK IS DONE, SHE TAKES NO CREDIT.
THAT IS WHY IT WILL LAST FOREVER.

IF YOU OVERLY ESTEEM TALENTED INDIVIDUALS,
PEOPLE WILL BECOME OVERLY COMPETITIVE.
IF YOU OVERVALUE POSSESSIONS,
PEOPLE WILL BEGIN TO STEAL.

DO NOT DISPLAY YOUR TREASURES
OR PEOPLE WILL BECOME ENVIOUS.
THE MASTER LEADS BY
EMPTYING PEOPLE'S MINDS;
FILLING THEIR BELLIES,
WEAKENING THEIR AMBITIONS,
AND MAKING THEM BECOME STRONG.

PREFERRING SIMPLICITY AND
FREEDOM FROM DESIRES,
AVOIDING THE PITFALLS OF KNOWLEDGE
AND WRONG ACTION.

FOR THOSE WHO PRACTICE NOT-DOING,
EVERYTHING WILL FALL INTO PLACE.

THE TAO IS LIKE AN EMPTY CONTAINER:
IT CAN NEVER BE EMPTIED
AND CAN NEVER BE FILLED.
INFINITELY DEEP, IT IS THE
SOURCE OF ALL THINGS.
IT DULLS THE SHARP, UNTIES THE KNOTTED,
SHADES THE LIGHTED, AND UNITES
ALL OF CREATION WITH DUST.

IT IS HIDDEN BUT ALWAYS PRESENT.
I DON'T KNOW WHO GAVE BIRTH TO IT .
IT IS OLDER THAN THE CONCEPT OF GOD.

HEAVEN AND EARTH ARE IMPARTIAL;
THEY TREAT ALL OF CREATION AS STRAW DOGS.
THE MASTER DOESN'T TAKE SIDES;
SHE TREATS EVERYONE LIKE A STRAW DOG.

THE SPACE BETWEEN HEAVEN AND EARTH IS LIKE A BELLOWS;
IT IS EMPTY, YET HAS NOT LOST ITS POWER.
THE MORE IT IS USED, THE MORE IT PRODUCES;
THE MORE YOU TALK OF IT, THE LESS YOU COMPREHEND.

IT IS BETTER NOT TO SPEAK OF THINGS
YOU DO NOT UNDERSTAND.

THE SPIRIT OF EMPTINESS IS IMMORTAL.
IT IS CALLED THE GREAT MOTHER
BECAUSE IT GIVES BIRTH TO HEAVEN AND EARTH.

IT IS LIKE A VAPOR,
BARELY SEEN BUT ALWAYS PRESENT.
USE IT EFFORTLESSLY.

THE TAO OF HEAVEN IS ETERNAL,
AND THE EARTH IS LONG ENDURING.
WHY ARE THEY LONG ENDURING?
THEY DO NOT LIVE FOR THEMSELVES;
THUS THEY ARE PRESENT FOR ALL BEINGS.

THE MASTER PUTS HERSELF LAST;
AND FINDS HERSELF IN THE PLACE OF AUTHORITY.
SHE DETACHES HERSELF FROM ALL THINGS;
THEREFORE SHE IS UNITED WITH ALL THINGS.
SHE GIVES NO THOUGHT TO SELF.
SHE IS PERFECTLY FULFILLED.

THE SUPREME GOOD IS LIKE WATER,
WHICH BENEFITS ALL OF CREATION
WITHOUT TRYING TO COMPETE WITH IT.
IT GATHERS IN UNPOPULAR PLACES.
THUS IT IS LIKE THE TAO.

THE LOCATION MAKES THE DWELLING GOOD.
DEPTH OF UNDERSTANDING MAKES THE MIND GOOD.
A KIND HEART MAKES THE GIVING GOOD.
INTEGRITY MAKES THE GOVERNMENT GOOD.
ACCOMPLISHMENTS MAKE YOUR LABORS GOOD.
PROPER TIMING MAKES A DECISION GOOD.

ONLY WHEN THERE IS NO COMPETITION
WILL WE ALL LIVE IN PEACE.

IT IS EASIER TO CARRY AN EMPTY CUP
THAN ONE THAT IS FILLED TO THE BRIM.

THE SHARPER THE KNIFE
THE EASIER IT IS TO DULL.
THE MORE WEALTH YOU POSSESS
THE HARDER IT IS TO PROTECT.
PRIDE BRINGS IT'S OWN TROUBLE.

WHEN YOU HAVE ACCOMPLISHED YOUR GOAL
SIMPLY WALK AWAY.
THIS IS THE PATHWAY TO HEAVEN.

NURTURE THE DARKNESS OF YOUR SOUL
UNTIL YOU BECOME WHOLE.
CAN YOU DO THIS AND NOT FAIL?
CAN YOU FOCUS YOUR LIFE-BREATH
UNTIL YOU BECOME
SUPPLE AS A NEWBORN CHILD?
WHILE YOU CLEANSE YOUR INNER VISION
WILL YOU BE FOUND WITHOUT FAULT?
CAN YOU LOVE PEOPLE AND LEAD THEM
WITHOUT FORCING YOUR WILL ON THEM?
WHEN HEAVEN GIVES AND TAKES AWAY
CAN YOU BE CONTENT WITH THE OUTCOME?
WHEN YOU UNDERSTAND ALL THINGS
CAN YOU STEP BACK FROM
YOUR OWN UNDERSTANDING?

GIVING BIRTH AND NOURISHING,
MAKING WITHOUT POSSESSING,
EXPECTING NOTHING IN RETURN.
TO GROW, YET NOT TO CONTROL:
THIS IS THE MYSTERIOUS VIRTUE.

THIRTY SPOKES ARE JOINED
TOGETHER IN A WHEEL,
BUT IT IS THE CENTER HOLE
THAT ALLOWS THE WHEEL TO
FUNCTION.

WE MOLD CLAY INTO A POT,
BUT IT IS THE EMPTINESS INSIDE
THAT MAKES THE VESSEL USEFUL.

WE FASHION WOOD FOR A HOUSE,
BUT IT IS THE EMPTINESS INSIDE
THAT MAKES IT LIVABLE.

WE WORK WITH THE SUBSTANTIAL,
BUT THE EMPTINESS IS WHAT WE
USE.

12

FIVE COLORS BLIND THE EYE.
FIVE NOTES DEAFEN THE EAR.
FIVE FLAVORS MAKE THE PALATE GO STALE.
TOO MUCH ACTIVITY DERANGES THE MIND.
TOO MUCH WEALTH CAUSES CRIME.

THE MASTER ACTS ON
WHAT SHE FEELS AND
NOT WHAT SHE SEES.
SHE SHUNS THE LATTER,
AND PREFERS
TO SEEK THE FORMER.

SUCCESS IS AS DANGEROUS AS FAILURE,
AND WE ARE OFTEN OUR OWN WORST ENEMY.

WHAT DOES IT MEAN THAT SUCCESS IS AS DANGEROUS AS FAILURE?
HE WHO IS SUPERIOR IS ALSO SOMEONE'S SUBORDINATE.
RECEIVING FAVOR AND LOSING IT BOTH CAUSE ALARM.
THAT IS WHAT IS MEANT BY SUCCESS IS AS DANGEROUS AS FAILURE.
WHAT DOES IT MEAN THAT WE ARE OFTEN OUR OWN WORST ENEMY?
THE REASON I HAVE AN ENEMY IS BECAUSE I HAVE "SELF".
IF I NO LONGER HAD A "SELF", I WOULD NO LONGER HAVE AN ENEMY.

LOVE THE WHOLE WORLD AS IF IT WERE YOUR SELF;
THEN YOU WILL TRULY CARE FOR ALL THINGS.

LOOK FOR IT, AND IT CAN'T BE SEEN.
LISTEN FOR IT, AND IT CAN'T BE HEARD.
GRASP FOR IT, AND IT CAN'T BE CAUGHT.
THESE THREE CANNOT BE FURTHER DESCRIBED,
SO WE TREAT THEM AS THE ONE.

IT'S HIGHEST IS NOT BRIGHT.
IT'S DEPTHS ARE NOT DARK.
UNENDING, UNNAMEABLE, IT RETURNS TO
NOTHINGNESS.
FORMLESS FORMS, AND IMAGE LESS IMAGES,
SUBTLE, BEYOND ALL UNDERSTANDING.

APPROACH IT AND YOU WILL NOT SEE A BEGINNING;
FOLLOW IT AND THERE WILL BE NO END.
WHEN WE GRASP THE TAO OF THE ANCIENT ONES,
WE CAN USE IT TO DIRECT OUR LIFE TODAY.
TO KNOW THE ANCIENT ORIGIN OF TAO:
THIS IS THE BEGINNING OF WISDOM.

THE SAGES OF OLD WERE PROFOUND
AND KNEW THE WAYS OF SUBTLETY AND DISCERNMENT.
THEIR WISDOM IS BEYOND OUR COMPREHENSION.
BECAUSE THEIR KNOWLEDGE WAS SO FAR SUPERIOR
I CAN ONLY GIVE A POOR DESCRIPTION.

THEY WERE CAREFUL
AS SOMEONE CROSSING A
FROZEN STREAM IN WINTER.
ALERT AS IF SURROUNDED
ON ALL SIDES BY THE ENEMY.
COURTEOUS AS A GUEST.
FLUID AS MELTING ICE.
WHOLE AS AN UNCARVED BLOCK OF WOOD.
RECEPTIVE AS A VALLEY.
TURBID AS MUDDIED WATER.

WHO CAN BE STILL
UNTIL THEIR MUD SETTLES
AND THE WATER IS CLEARED BY ITSELF?
CAN YOU REMAIN TRANQUIL UNTIL
RIGHT ACTION OCCURS BY ITSELF?

THE MASTER DOESN'T SEEK FULFILLMENT.
FOR ONLY THOSE WHO ARE NOT FULL
ARE ABLE TO BE USED
WHICH BRINGS THE FEELING OF COMPLETENESS.

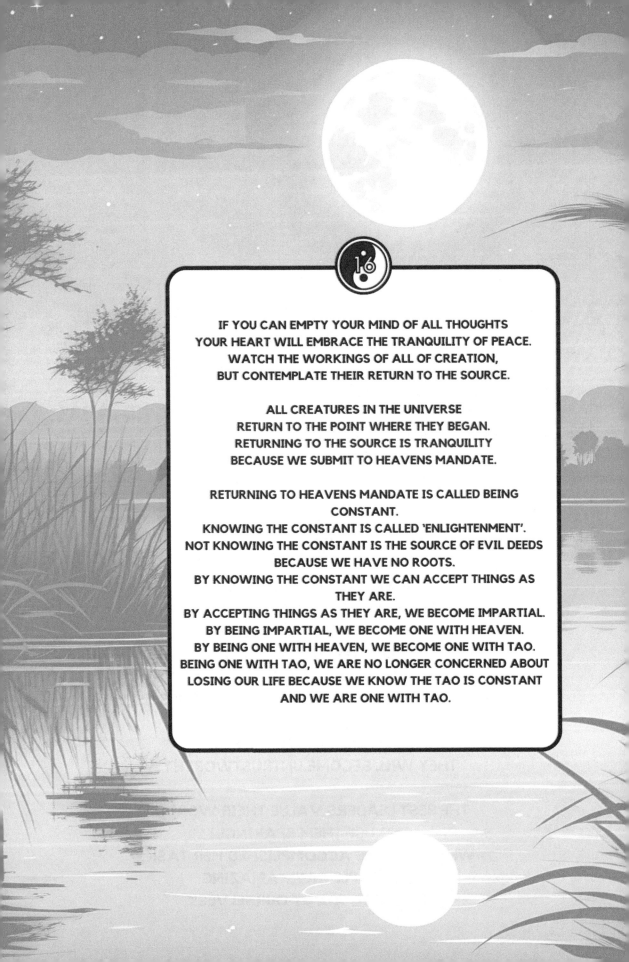

IF YOU CAN EMPTY YOUR MIND OF ALL THOUGHTS
YOUR HEART WILL EMBRACE THE TRANQUILITY OF PEACE.
WATCH THE WORKINGS OF ALL OF CREATION,
BUT CONTEMPLATE THEIR RETURN TO THE SOURCE.

ALL CREATURES IN THE UNIVERSE
RETURN TO THE POINT WHERE THEY BEGAN.
RETURNING TO THE SOURCE IS TRANQUILITY
BECAUSE WE SUBMIT TO HEAVENS MANDATE.

RETURNING TO HEAVENS MANDATE IS CALLED BEING
CONSTANT.
KNOWING THE CONSTANT IS CALLED 'ENLIGHTENMENT'.
NOT KNOWING THE CONSTANT IS THE SOURCE OF EVIL DEEDS
BECAUSE WE HAVE NO ROOTS.
BY KNOWING THE CONSTANT WE CAN ACCEPT THINGS AS
THEY ARE.
BY ACCEPTING THINGS AS THEY ARE, WE BECOME IMPARTIAL.
BY BEING IMPARTIAL, WE BECOME ONE WITH HEAVEN.
BY BEING ONE WITH HEAVEN, WE BECOME ONE WITH TAO.
BEING ONE WITH TAO, WE ARE NO LONGER CONCERNED ABOUT
LOSING OUR LIFE BECAUSE WE KNOW THE TAO IS CONSTANT
AND WE ARE ONE WITH TAO.

THE BEST LEADERS ARE THOSE
THE PEOPLE HARDLY KNOW EXIST.
THE NEXT BEST IS A LEADER
WHO IS LOVED AND PRAISED.
NEXT COMES THE ONE WHO IS FEARED.
THE WORST ONE IS THE LEADER THAT IS DESPISED.

IF YOU DON'T TRUST THE PEOPLE,
THEY WILL BECOME UNTRUSTWORTHY.

THE BEST LEADERS VALUE THEIR WORDS,
AND USE THEM SPARINGLY.
WHEN SHE HAS ACCOMPLISHED HER TASK,
THE PEOPLE SAY, "AMAZING:
WE DID IT, ALL BY OURSELVES!"

WHEN THE GREAT TAO IS ABANDONED,
CHARITY AND RIGHTEOUSNESS APPEAR.
WHEN INTELLECTUALISM ARISES,
HYPOCRISY IS CLOSE BEHIND.

WHEN THERE IS STRIFE IN THE FAMILY UNIT,
PEOPLE TALK ABOUT 'BROTHERLY LOVE'.

WHEN THE COUNTRY FALLS INTO CHAOS,
POLITICIANS TALK ABOUT 'PATRIOTISM'.

FORGET ABOUT
KNOWLEDGE AND WISDOM,
AND PEOPLE WILL BE A
HUNDRED TIMES BETTER OFF.
THROW AWAY
CHARITY AND
RIGHTEOUSNESS,
AND PEOPLE WILL
RETURN TO BROTHERLY LOVE.
THROW AWAY
PROFIT AND GREED,
AND THERE WON'T BE ANY
THIEVES.

THESE THREE ARE SUPERFICIAL
AND AREN'T ENOUGH
TO KEEP US AT THE CENTER OF
THE CIRCLE,
SO WE MUST ALSO:

EMBRACE SIMPLICITY.
PUT OTHERS FIRST.
DESIRE LITTLE.

RENOUNCE KNOWLEDGE AND YOUR PROBLEMS WILL END.
WHAT IS THE DIFFERENCE BETWEEN YES AND NO?
WHAT IS THE DIFFERENCE BETWEEN GOOD AND EVIL?
MUST YOU FEAR WHAT OTHERS FEAR?
NONSENSE, LOOK HOW FAR YOU HAVE MISSED THE MARK!
OTHER PEOPLE ARE JOYOUS,
AS THOUGH THEY WERE AT A SPRING FESTIVAL.
I ALONE AM UNCONCERNED AND EXPRESSIONLESS,
LIKE AN INFANT BEFORE IT HAS LEARNED TO SMILE.
OTHER PEOPLE HAVE MORE THAN THEY NEED;
I ALONE SEEM TO POSSESS NOTHING.
I AM LOST AND DRIFT ABOUT WITH NO PLACE TO GO.

I AM LIKE A FOOL; MY MIND IS IN CHAOS.
ORDINARY PEOPLE ARE BRIGHT;I ALONE AM DARK.
ORDINARY PEOPLE ARE CLEVER;I ALONE AM DULL.
ORDINARY PEOPLE SEEM DISCRIMINATING;
I ALONE AM MUDDLED AND CONFUSED.
I DRIFT ON THE WAVES ON THE OCEAN,
BLOWN AT THE MERCY OF THE WIND.
OTHER PEOPLE HAVE THEIR GOALS,
I ALONE AM DULL AND UNCOUTH.
I AM DIFFERENT FROM ORDINARY PEOPLE.
I NURSE FROM THE GREAT MOTHER'S BREASTS.

21

THE GREATEST VIRTUE YOU CAN HAVE
COMES FROM FOLLOWING ONLY THE TAO;
WHICH TAKES A FORM THAT
IS INTANGIBLE AND EVASIVE.

EVEN THOUGH THE TAO IS
INTANGIBLE AND EVASIVE,
WE ARE ABLE TO KNOW IT EXISTS.
INTANGIBLE AND EVASIVE,
YET IT HAS A MANIFESTATION.
SECLUDED AND DARK,
YET THERE IS A VITALITY WITHIN IT.
ITS VITALITY IS VERY GENUINE.
WITHIN IT WE CAN FIND ORDER.

SINCE THE BEGINNING OF TIME,
THE TAO HAS ALWAYS EXISTED.
IT IS BEYOND EXISTING AND
NOT EXISTING.
HOW DO I KNOW WHERE
CREATION COMES FROM?
I LOOK INSIDE MYSELF AND
SEE IT.

IF YOU WANT TO BECOME WHOLE,
FIRST LET YOURSELF BECOME BROKEN.
IF YOU WANT TO BECOME STRAIGHT,
FIRST LET YOURSELF BECOME TWISTED.
IF YOU WANT TO BECOME FULL,
FIRST LET YOURSELF BECOME EMPTY.
IF YOU WANT TO BECOME NEW,
FIRST LET YOURSELF BECOME OLD.
THOSE WHOSE DESIRES ARE FEW GETS THEM,
THOSE WHOSE DESIRES ARE GREAT GO ASTRAY.

FOR THIS REASON THE MASTER EMBRACES THE TAO,
AS AN EXAMPLE FOR THE WORLD TO FOLLOW.
BECAUSE SHE ISN'T SELF CENTERED,
PEOPLE CAN SEE THE LIGHT IN HER.
BECAUSE SHE DOES NOT BOAST OF HERSELF,
SHE BECOMES A SHINING EXAMPLE.
BECAUSE SHE DOES NOT GLORIFY HERSELF,
SHE BECOMES A PERSON OF MERIT.
BECAUSE SHE WANTS NOTHING FROM THE WORLD,
THE WORLD CANNOT OVERCOME HER.

WHEN THE ANCIENT MASTERS SAID,
"IF YOU WANT TO BECOME WHOLE,
THEN FIRST LET YOURSELF BE BROKEN,"
THEY WEREN'T USING EMPTY WORDS.
ALL WHO DO THIS WILL BE MADE COMPLETE.

NATURE USES FEW WORDS:
WHEN THE GALE BLOWS, IT WILL NOT LAST LONG;
WHEN IT RAINS HARD, IT LASTS BUT A LITTLE WHILE;
WHAT CAUSES THESE TO HAPPEN? HEAVEN AND EARTH.

WHY DO WE HUMANS GO ON ENDLESSLY ABOUT LITTLE
WHEN NATURE DOES MUCH IN A LITTLE TIME?
IF YOU OPEN YOURSELF TO THE TAO,
YOU AND TAO BECOME ONE.
IF YOU OPEN YOURSELF TO VIRTUE,
THEN YOU CAN BECOME VIRTUOUS.
IF YOU OPEN YOURSELF TO LOSS,
THEN YOU WILL BECOME LOST.

IF YOU OPEN YOURSELF TO THE TAO,
THE TAO WILL EAGERLY WELCOME YOU.
IF YOU OPEN YOURSELF TO VIRTUE,
VIRTUE WILL BECOME A PART OF YOU.
IF YOU OPEN YOURSELF TO LOSS,
THE LOST ARE GLAD TO SEE YOU.

"WHEN YOU DO NOT TRUST PEOPLE,
PEOPLE WILL BECOME UNTRUSTWORTHY."

THOSE WHO STAND ON TIPTOES
DO NOT STAND FIRMLY.
THOSE WHO RUSH AHEAD
DON'T GET VERY FAR.
THOSE WHO TRY TO OUT SHINE OTHERS
DIM THEIR OWN LIGHT.
THOSE WHO CALL THEMSELVES RIGHTEOUS
CAN'T KNOW HOW WRONG THEY ARE.
THOSE WHO BOAST OF THEIR ACCOMPLISHMENTS
DIMINISHES THE THINGS THEY HAVE DONE.

COMPARED TO THE TAO,
THESE ACTIONS ARE UNWORTHY.
IF WE ARE TO FOLLOW THE TAO,
WE MUST NOT DO THESE THINGS.

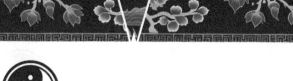

BEFORE THE UNIVERSE WAS BORN
THERE WAS SOMETHING IN THE CHAOS OF THE HEAVENS.
IT STANDS ALONE AND EMPTY,
SOLITARY AND UNCHANGING.
IT IS EVER PRESENT AND SECURE.
IT MAY BE REGARDED AS THE MOTHER OF THE UNIVERSE.
BECAUSE I DO NOT KNOW IT'S NAME,
I CALL IT THE TAO.
IF FORCED TO GIVE IT A NAME,
I WOULD CALL IT 'GREAT'.

BECAUSE IT IS GREAT MEANS IT IS EVERYWHERE.
BEING EVERYWHERE MEANS IT IS ETERNAL.
BEING ETERNAL MEANS EVERYTHING RETURNS TO IT.

TAO IS GREAT. HEAVEN IS GREAT.
EARTH IS GREAT. HUMANITY IS GREAT.
WITHIN THE UNIVERSE, THESE ARE THE FOUR GREAT THINGS.

HUMANITY FOLLOWS THE EARTH.
EARTH FOLLOWS HEAVEN.
HEAVEN FOLLOWS THE TAO.
THE TAO FOLLOWS ONLY ITSELF.

HEAVINESS IS THE BASIS OF LIGHTNESS.
STILLNESS IS THE STANDARD OF ACTIVITY.

THUS THE MASTER TRAVELS ALL DAY
WITHOUT EVER LEAVING HER WAGON.
EVEN THOUGH SHE HAS MUCH TO SEE,
IS SHE AT PEACE IN HER INDIFFERENCE.

WHY SHOULD THE LORD OF A THOUSAND CHARIOTS
BE AMUSED AT THE FOOLISHNESS OF THE WORLD?
IF YOU ABANDON YOURSELF TO FOOLISHNESS,
YOU LOSE TOUCH WITH YOUR BEGINNINGS.
IF YOU LET YOURSELF BECOME DISTRACTED,
YOU WILL LOSE THE BASIS OF YOUR POWER.

A GOOD TRAVELER LEAVES NO
TRACKS,
AND A SKILLFUL SPEAKER IS WELL
REHEARSED.
A GOOD BOOKKEEPER HAS AN
EXCELLENT MEMORY,
AND A WELL-MADE DOOR IS EASY
TO OPEN AND NEEDS NO LOCKS.
A GOOD KNOT NEEDS NO ROPE
AND IT CANNOT COME UNDONE.
THUS THE MASTER IS WILLING TO
HELP EVERYONE,
AND DOESN'T KNOW THE
MEANING OF REJECTION.
SHE IS THERE TO HELP ALL OF
CREATION,
AND DOESN'T ABANDON EVEN THE
SMALLEST CREATURE.
THIS IS CALLED EMBRACING THE
LIGHT.

WHAT IS A GOOD PERSON BUT A
BAD PERSON'S TEACHER?
WHAT IS A BAD PERSON BUT RAW
MATERIEL FOR HIS TEACHER?
IF YOU FAIL TO HONOR YOUR
TEACHER OR FAIL TO ENJOY YOUR
STUDENT,
YOU WILL BECOME DELUDED NO
MATTER HOW SMART YOU ARE.
IT IS THE SECRET OF PRIME
IMPORTANCE.

KNOW THE MASCULINE, BUT KEEP TO THE FEMININE:
AND BECOME A WATERSHED TO THE WORLD.
IF YOU EMBRACE THE WORLD, THE TAO WILL NEVER LEAVE YOU
AND YOU BECOME AS A LITTLE CHILD.

KNOW THE WHITE, YET KEEP TO THE BLACK:
BE A MODEL FOR THE WORLD.
IF YOU ARE A MODEL FOR THE WORLD,
THE TAO INSIDE YOU WILL STRENGTHEN
AND YOU WILL RETURN WHOLE
TO YOUR ETERNAL BEGINNING.

KNOW THE HONORABLE, BUT DO NOT SHUN THE DISGRACED:
EMBRACING THE WORLD AS IT IS.
IF YOU EMBRACE THE WORLD WITH COMPASSION,
THEN YOUR VIRTUE WILL RETURN YOU TO THE UNCARVED BLOCK.

THE BLOCK OF WOOD IS CARVED INTO UTENSILS
BY CARVING VOID INTO THE WOOD.
THE MASTER USES THE UTENSILS, YET PREFERS TO KEEP TO THE BLOCK
BECAUSE OF ITS LIMITLESS POSSIBILITIES.
GREAT WORKS DO NOT INVOLVE DISCARDING SUBSTANCE.

DO YOU WANT TO RULE THE
WORLD AND CONTROL IT?
I DON'T THINK IT CAN EVER BE DONE.

THE WORLD IS SACRED VESSEL
AND IT CANNOT BE CONTROLLED.
YOU WILL ONLY IT MAKE IT WORSE IF YOU TRY.
IT MAY SLIP THROUGH YOUR
FINGERS AND DISAPPEAR.

SOME ARE MEANT TO LEAD,
AND OTHERS ARE MEANT TO FOLLOW;
SOME MUST ALWAYS STRAIN,
AND OTHERS HAVE AN EASY TIME;
SOME ARE NATURALLY BIG AND STRONG,
AND OTHERS WILL ALWAYS BE SMALL;
SOME WILL BE PROTECTED AND NURTURED,
AND OTHERS WILL MEET WITH DESTRUCTION.

THE MASTER ACCEPTS THINGS AS THEY ARE,
AND OUT OF COMPASSION AVOIDS
EXTRAVAGANCE, EXCESS AND THE EXTREMES.

THOSE WHO LEAD PEOPLE BY FOLLOWING THE
TAO
DON'T USE WEAPONS TO ENFORCE THEIR WILL.
USING FORCE ALWAYS LEADS TO UNSEEN
TROUBLES.
IN THE PLACES WHERE ARMIES MARCH,
THORNS AND BRIARS BLOOM AND GROW.
AFTER ARMIES TAKE TO WAR,
BAD YEARS MUST ALWAYS FOLLOW.
THE SKILLFUL COMMANDER
STRIKES A DECISIVE BLOW THEN STOPS.
WHEN VICTORY IS WON OVER THE ENEMY
THROUGH WAR
IT IS NOT A THING OF GREAT PRIDE.
WHEN THE BATTLE IS OVER,
ARROGANCE IS THE NEW ENEMY.
WAR CAN RESULT WHEN NO OTHER
ALTERNATIVE IS GIVEN,
SO THE ONE WHO OVERCOMES AN ENEMY
SHOULD NOT DOMINATE THEM.
THE STRONG ALWAYS WEAKENED WITH
TIME.

THIS IS NOT THE WAY OF THE TAO.
THAT WHICH IS NOT OF THE TAO WILL SOON
END.

31

WEAPONS ARE THE BEARERS OF BAD NEWS;
ALL PEOPLE SHOULD DETEST THEM.

THE WISE MAN VALUES THE LEFT SIDE,
AND IN TIME OF WAR HE VALUES THE RIGHT.
WEAPONS ARE MEANT FOR DESTRUCTION,
AND THUS ARE AVOIDED BY THE WISE.
ONLY AS A LAST RESORT
WILL A WISE PERSON USE A DEADLY WEAPON.
IF PEACE IS HIS TRUE OBJECTIVE.
HOW CAN HE REJOICE IN THE VICTORY OF WAR?
THOSE WHO REJOICE IN VICTORY
DELIGHT IN THE SLAUGHTER OF HUMANITY.
THOSE WHO RESORT TO VIOLENCE
WILL NEVER BRING PEACE TO THE WORLD.
THE LEFT SIDE IS A PLACE OF HONOR
ON HAPPY OCCASIONS.
THE RIGHT SIDE IS RESERVED FOR
MOURNING AT A FUNERAL.
WHEN THE LIEUTENANTS TAKE THE LEFT
SIDE TO PREPARE FOR WAR,
THE GENERAL SHOULD BE ON THE RIGHT SIDE,
BECAUSE HE KNOWS THE OUTCOME WILL BE DEATH.
THE DEATH OF MANY SHOULD BE
GREETED WITH GREAT SORROW,
AND THE VICTORY CELEBRATION SHOULD
HONOR THOSE WHO HAVE DIED.

32

THE TAO IS NAMELESS AND UNCHANGING.
ALTHOUGH IT APPEARS INSIGNIFICANT,
NOTHING IN THE WORLD CAN CONTAIN IT.

IF A RULER ABIDES BY ITS PRINCIPLES,
THEN HER PEOPLE WILL WILLINGLY FOLLOW.
HEAVEN WOULD THEN REIGN ON EARTH,
LIKE SWEET RAIN FALLING ON PARADISE.
PEOPLE WOULD HAVE NO NEED FOR LAWS,
BECAUSE THE LAW WOULD BE
WRITTEN ON THEIR HEARTS.

NAMING IS A NECESSITY FOR ORDER,
BUT NAMING CANNOT ORDER ALL THINGS.
NAMING OFTEN MAKES
THINGS IMPERSONAL,
SO WE SHOULD KNOW
WHEN NAMING SHOULD END.
KNOWING WHEN TO STOP NAMING,
YOU CAN AVOID THE PITFALL IT BRINGS.

ALL THINGS END IN THE TAO
JUST AS THE SMALL STREAMS
AND THE LARGEST RIVERS
FLOW THROUGH VALLEYS TO THE SEA.

33

THOSE WHO KNOW OTHERS ARE INTELLIGENT;
THOSE WHO KNOW THEMSELVES ARE TRULY WISE.
THOSE WHO MASTER OTHERS ARE STRONG;
THOSE WHO MASTER THEMSELVES HAVE TRUE POWER.

THOSE WHO KNOW THEY
HAVE ENOUGH ARE TRULY WEALTHY.

THOSE WHO PERSIST WILL REACH THEIR GOAL.

THOSE WHO KEEP THEIR COURSE HAVE A STRONG WILL.
THOSE WHO EMBRACE DEATH WILL NOT PERISH,
BUT HAVE LIFE EVERLASTING.

THE GREAT TAO FLOWS UNOBSTRUCTED
IN EVERY DIRECTION.
ALL THINGS RELY ON IT
TO CONCEIVE AND BE BORN,
AND IT DOES NOT DENY
EVEN THE SMALLEST OF CREATION.
WHEN IT HAS ACCOMPLISHES GREAT WONDERS,
IT DOES NOT CLAIM THEM FOR ITSELF.
IT NOURISHES INFINITE WORLDS,
YET IT DOESN'T SEEK TO
MASTER THE SMALLEST CREATURE.
SINCE IT IS WITHOUT WANTS AND DESIRES,
IT CAN BE CONSIDERED HUMBLE.
ALL OF CREATION SEEKS IT FOR REFUGE
YET IT DOES NOT SEEK TO MASTER OR CONTROL.
BECAUSE IT DOES NOT SEEK GREATNESS;
IT IS ABLE TO ACCOMPLISH TRULY GREAT THINGS.

35

SHE WHO FOLLOWS THE WAY OF THE TAO
WILL DRAW THE WORLD TO HER STEPS.
SHE CAN GO WITHOUT FEAR OF BEING INJURED,
BECAUSE SHE HAS FOUND PEACE
AND TRANQUILITY IN HER HEART.

WHERE THERE IS MUSIC AND GOOD FOOD,
PEOPLE WILL STOP TO ENJOY IT.
BUT WORDS SPOKEN OF THE TAO
SEEM TO THEM BORING AND STALE.
WHEN LOOKED AT, THERE IS NOTHING FOR THEM TO SEE.
WHEN LISTEN FOR, THERE IS NOTHING FOR THEM TO HEAR.
YET IF THEY PUT IT TO USE, IT WOULD NEVER BE EXHAUSTED.

IF YOU WANT SOMETHING
TO RETURN TO THE SOURCE,
YOU MUST FIRST ALLOW
IT TO SPREAD OUT.
IF YOU WANT SOMETHING TO WEAKEN,
YOU MUST FIRST ALLOW
IT TO BECOME STRONG.
IF YOU WANT SOMETHING TO BE REMOVED,
YOU MUST FIRST ALLOW IT TO FLOURISH.
IF YOU WANT TO POSSESS SOMETHING,
YOU MUST FIRST GIVE IT AWAY.

THIS IS CALLED THE
SUBTLE UNDERSTANDING
OF HOW THINGS ARE MEANT TO BE.
THE SOFT AND PLIABLE OVERCOMES
THE HARD AND INFLEXIBLE.

JUST AS FISH REMAIN
HIDDEN IN DEEP WATERS,
IT IS BEST TO KEEP
WEAPONS OUT OF SIGHT.

THE TAO NEVER ACTS WITH FORCE,
YET THERE IS NOTHING THAT IT CANNOT DO.

IF RULERS COULD FOLLOW THE WAY OF THE TAO,
THEN ALL OF CREATION WOULD WILLINGLY FOLLOW THEIR EXAMPLE.
IF SELFISH DESIRES WERE TO ARISE AFTER THEIR TRANSFORMATION,
I WOULD ERASE THEM WITH THE POWER OF THE UNCARVED BLOCK.

BY THE POWER OF THE UNCARVED BLOCK,
FUTURE GENERATIONS WOULD LOOSE THEIR SELFISH DESIRES.
BY LOSING THEIR SELFISH DESIRES, THE WORLD WOULD NATURALLY
SETTLE INTO PEACE.

38

THE HIGHEST GOOD IS NOT TO SEEK TO DO GOOD,
BUT TO ALLOW YOURSELF TO BECOME IT.
THE ORDINARY PERSON SEEKS TO DO GOOD
THINGS,
AND FINDS THAT THEY CANNOT DO THEM
CONTINUALLY.

THE MASTER DOES NOT FORCE VIRTUE ON
OTHERS,
THUS SHE IS ABLE TO ACCOMPLISH HER TASK.
THE ORDINARY PERSON WHO USES FORCE,
WILL FIND THAT THEY ACCOMPLISH NOTHING.

THE KIND PERSON ACTS FROM THE HEART,
AND ACCOMPLISHES A MULTITUDE OF THINGS.
THE RIGHTEOUS PERSON ACTS OUT OF PITY,
YET LEAVES MANY THINGS UNDONE.
THE MORAL PERSON WILL ACT OUT OF DUTY,
AND WHEN NO ONE WILL RESPOND
WILL ROLL UP HIS SLEEVES AND USES FORCE.

WHEN THE TAO IS FORGOTTEN, THERE IS
RIGHTEOUSNESS.
WHEN RIGHTEOUSNESS IS FORGOTTEN, THERE IS
MORALITY.
WHEN MORALITY IS FORGOTTEN, THERE IS THE
LAW.
THE LAW IS THE HUSK OF FAITH,
AND TRUST IS THE BEGINNING OF CHAOS.

OUR BASIC UNDERSTANDINGS ARE NOT FROM
THE TAO
BECAUSE THEY COME FROM THE DEPTHS OF OUR
MISUNDERSTANDING.
THE MASTER ABIDES IN THE FRUIT AND NOT IN
THE HUSK.
SHE DWELLS IN THE TAO, AND NOT WITH THE
THINGS THAT HIDE IT.
THIS IS HOW SHE INCREASES IN WISDOM.

THE MASTERS OF OLD ATTAINED UNITY WITH THE
TAO.
HEAVEN ATTAINED UNITY AND BECOME PURE.
THE EARTH ATTAINED UNITY AND FOUND PEACE.
THE SPIRITS ATTAINED UNITY SO THEY COULD
MINISTER.
THE VALLEYS ATTAINED UNITY THAT THEY MIGHT BE
FULL.
HUMANITY ATTAINED UNITY THAT THEY MIGHT
FLOURISH.
THEIR LEADERS ATTAINED UNITY THAT THEY MIGHT
SET THE EXAMPLE.
THIS IS THE POWER OF UNITY.

WITHOUT UNITY, THE SKY BECOMES FILTHY.
WITHOUT UNITY, THE EARTH BECOMES UNSTABLE.
WITHOUT UNITY, THE SPIRITS BECOME
UNRESPONSIVE AND DISAPPEAR.
WITHOUT UNITY, THE VALLEYS BECOME DRY AS A
DESERT.
WITHOUT UNITY, HUMAN KIND CAN'T
REPRODUCE AND BECOMES EXTINCT.
WITHOUT UNITY, OUR LEADERS BECOME CORRUPT AND
FALL.

THE GREAT VIEW THE SMALL AS THEIR SOURCE,
AND THE HIGH TAKES THE LOW AS THEIR
FOUNDATION.
THEIR GREATEST ASSET BECOMES THEIR HUMILITY.
THEY SPEAK OF THEMSELVES AS ORPHANS AND
WIDOWS,
THUS THEY TRULY SEEK HUMILITY.
DO NOT SHINE LIKE THE PRECIOUS GEM,
BUT BE AS DULL AS A COMMON STONE.

ALL MOVEMENT RETURNS TO THE TAO.
WEAKNESS IS HOW THE TAO WORKS.

ALL OF CREATION IS BORN FROM SUBSTANCE.
SUBSTANCE IS BORN OF NOTHING-NESS.

41

WHEN A SUPERIOR PERSON HEARS OF THE TAO,
SHE DILIGENTLY PUTS IT INTO PRACTICE.
WHEN AN AVERAGE PERSON HEARS OF THE TAO,
HE BELIEVES HALF OF IT, AND DOUBTS THE OTHER HALF.
WHEN A FOOLISH PERSON HEARS OF THE TAO,
HE LAUGHS OUT LOUD AT THE VERY IDEA.
IF HE DIDN'T LAUGH,
IT WOULDN'T BE THE TAO.

THUS IT IS SAID:
THE BRIGHTNESS OF THE TAO SEEMS LIKE DARKNESS,
THE ADVANCEMENT OF THE TAO SEEMS LIKE RETREAT,
THE LEVEL PATH SEEMS ROUGH,
THE SUPERIOR PATH SEEM EMPTY,
THE PURE SEEMS TO BE TARNISHED,
AND TRUE VIRTUE DOESN'T SEEM TO BE ENOUGH.

THE VIRTUE OF CAUTION SEEMS LIKE COWARDICE,
THE PURE SEEMS TO BE POLLUTED, THE TRUE SQUARE SEEMS
TO HAVE NO CORNERS, THE BEST VESSELS TAKE
THE MOST TIME TO FINISH, THE GREATEST SOUNDS
CANNOT BE HEARD, AND THE GREATEST IMAGE HAS NO FORM.

THE TAO HIDES IN THE UNNAMED,
YET IT ALONE NOURISHES
AND COMPLETES ALL THINGS.

THE TAO GAVE BIRTH TO ONE.
THE ONE GAVE BIRTH TO TWO.
THE TWO GAVE BIRTH TO THREE.
THE THREE GAVE BIRTH TO ALL OF
CREATION.

ALL THINGS CARRY YIN YET EMBRACE
YANG.
THEY BLEND THEIR LIFE BREATHS
IN ORDER TO PRODUCE HARMONY.

PEOPLE DESPISE BEING ORPHANED,
WIDOWED AND POOR.
BUT THE NOBLE ONES TAKE THESE AS
THEIR TITLES.
IN LOSING, MUCH IS GAINED,
AND IN GAINING, MUCH IS LOST.

WHAT OTHERS TEACH I TOO WILL TEACH:
"THE STRONG AND VIOLENT WILL
NOT DIE A NATURAL DEATH."

THAT WHICH OFFERS NO RESISTANCE,
OVERCOMES THE HARDEST SUBSTANCES.
THAT WHICH OFFERSNO RESISTANCE
CAN ENTER WHERE THERE IS NO SPACE.

FEW IN THE WORLD
CAN COMPREHEND
THE TEACHING WITHOUT WORDS,
OR UNDERSTAND THE VALUE
OF NON-ACTION.

WHICH IS MORE IMPORTANT,
YOUR HONOR OR YOUR LIFE?
WHICH IS MORE VALUABLE,
YOUR POSSESSIONS OR YOUR PERSON?
WHICH IS MORE DESTRUCTIVE,
SUCCESS OR FAILURE?

BECAUSE OF THIS, GREAT LOVE EXTRACTS A GREAT COST
AND TRUE WEALTH REQUIRES GREATER LOSS.

KNOWING WHEN YOU HAVE ENOUGH
AVOIDS DISHONOR,
AND KNOWING WHEN TO STOP
WILL KEEP YOU FROM DANGER
AND BRING YOU A LONG, HAPPY LIFE.

THE GREATEST ACCOMPLISHMENTS SEEM IMPERFECT,
YET THEIR USEFULNESS IS NOT DIMINISHED.
THE GREATEST FULLNESS SEEMS EMPTY,
YET IT WILL BE INEXHAUSTIBLE.

THE GREATEST STRAIGHTNESS SEEMS CROOKED.
THE MOST VALUED SKILL SEEMS LIKE CLUMSINESS.
THE GREATEST SPEECH SEEMS FULL OF STAMMERS.

MOVEMENT OVERCOMES THE COLD,
AND STILLNESS OVERCOMES THE HEAT.
THAT WHICH IS PURE AND STILL IS THE UNIVERSAL IDEAL.

WHEN THE WORLD
FOLLOWS THE TAO,
HORSES RUN FREE
TO FERTILIZE THE FIELDS.

WHEN THE WORLD
DOES NOT FOLLOW THE TAO,
WAR HORSES ARE
BREAD OUTSIDE THE CITIES.

THERE IS NO GREATER
TRANSGRESSION THAN CONDONING
PEOPLES SELFISH DESIRES,
NO GREATER DISASTER
THAN BEING DISCONTENT,
AND NO GREATER
RETRIBUTION THAN FOR GREED.

WHOEVER KNOWS CONTENTMENT
WILL BE AT PEACE FOREVER.

WITHOUT OPENING YOUR DOOR,
YOU CAN KNOW THE WHOLE WORLD.
WITHOUT LOOKING OUT YOUR WINDOW,
YOU CAN UNDERSTAND THE WAY OF THE TAO.

THE MORE KNOWLEDGE YOU SEEK,
THE LESS YOU WILL UNDERSTAND.

THE MASTER UNDERSTANDS WITHOUT LEAVING,
SEES CLEARLY WITHOUT LOOKING,
ACCOMPLISHES MUCH WITHOUT DOING ANYTHING.

ONE WHO SEEKS KNOWLEDGE
LEARNS SOMETHING NEW EVERY DAY.
ONE WHO SEEKS THE TAO
UNLEARNS SOMETHING NEW EVERY DAY.
LESS AND LESS REMAINS UNTIL
YOU ARRIVE AT NON-ACTION.
WHEN YOU ARRIVE AT NON-ACTION,
NOTHING WILL BE LEFT UNDONE.

MASTERY OF THE WORLD IS ACHIEVED
BY LETTING THINGS TAKE THEIR NATURAL COURSE.
YOU CANNOT MASTER THE WORLD
BY CHANGING THE NATURAL WAY.

THE MASTER HAS NO
MIND OF HER OWN.
SHE UNDERSTANDS
THE MIND OF THE PEOPLE.

TO THOSE WHO ARE GOOD
SHE TREATS AS GOOD.
TO THOSE WHO AREN'T GOOD
SHE ALSO TREATS AS GOOD.
THIS IS HOW SHE ATTAINS
TRUE GOODNESS.

SHE TRUSTS PEOPLE
WHO ARE TRUSTWORTHY.
SHE ALSO TRUSTS PEOPLE
WHO AREN'T TRUSTWORTHY.
THIS IS HOW SHE GAINS TRUE TRUST.

THE MASTER'S MIND IS
SHUT OFF FROM THE WORLD.
ONLY FOR THE SAKE OF THE
PEOPLE DOES SHE MUDDLE HER MIND.
THEY LOOK TO HER IN ANTICIPATION.
YET SHE TREATS THEM ALL AS HER
CHILDREN.

THOSE WHO LEAVE THE WOMB AT BIRTH
AND THOSE WHO ENTER THEIR SOURCE
AT DEATH,
OF THESE; THREE OUT OF TEN CELEBRATE
LIFE,
THREE OUT OF TEN CELEBRATE DEATH,
AND THREE OUT OF TEN SIMPLY
GO FROM LIFE TO DEATH.
WHAT IS THE REASON FOR THIS?
BECAUSE THEY ARE AFRAID OF DYING,
THEREFORE THEY CANNOT LIVE.

I HAVE HEARD THAT THOSE
WHO CELEBRATE LIFE
WALK SAFELY AMONG
THE WILD ANIMALS.
WHEN THEY GO INTO BATTLE,
THEY REMAIN UNHARMED.
THE ANIMALS FIND NO
PLACE TO ATTACK THEM
AND THE WEAPONS ARE
UNABLE TO HARM THEM.
WHY? BECAUSE THEY CAN FIND
NO PLACE FOR DEATH IN THEM.

51

THE TAO GIVES BIRTH TO ALL OF CREATION.
THE VIRTUE OF TAO IN NATURE NURTURES THEM,
AND THEIR FAMILY GIVE THEM THEIR FORM.
THEIR ENVIRONMENT THENSHAPES THEM INTO COMPLETION.
THAT IS WHY EVERY CREATURE
HONORS THE TAO AND ITS VIRTUE.

NO ONE TELLS THEM TO HONOR THE TAO AND ITS VIRTUE,
IT HAPPENS ALL BY ITSELF.SO THE TAO GIVES THEM BIRTH,
AND ITS VIRTUE CULTIVATES THEM,CARES FOR THEM,
NURTURES THEM,GIVES THEM A PLACE OF REFUGE AND PEACE,
HELPS THEM TO GROW AND SHELTERS THEM.

IT GIVES THEM LIFE WITHOUTWANTING TO POSSES THEM,
AND CARES FOR THEM EXPECTING NOTHING IN RETURN.
IT IS THEIR MASTER, BUT IT DOES NOT SEEK TO DOMINATE
THEM.
THIS IS CALLED THE DARK AND MYSTERIOUS VIRTUE.

52

THE WORLD HAD A BEGINNING
WHICH WE CALL THE GREAT MOTHER.
ONCE WE HAVE FOUND THE MOTHER,
WE BEGIN TO KNOW WHAT
HER CHILDREN SHOULD BE.

WHEN WE KNOW WE ARE THE MOTHERS CHILD,
WE BEGIN TO GUARD THE QUALITIES
OF THE MOTHER IN US.
SHE WILL PROTECT US FROM ALL DANGER
EVEN IF WE LOSE OUR LIFE.

KEEP YOUR MOUTH CLOSED
AND EMBRACE A SIMPLE LIFE,
AND YOU WILL LIVE CARE-FREE
UNTIL THE END OF YOUR DAYS.
IF YOU TRY TO TALK YOUR WAY INTO A BETTER LIFE
THERE WILL BE NO END TO YOUR TROUBLE.

TO UNDERSTAND THE SMALL IS CALLED CLARITY.
KNOWING HOW TO YIELD IS CALLED STRENGTH.
TO USE YOUR INNER LIGHT FOR UNDERSTANDING
REGARDLESS OF THE DANGER
IS CALLED DEPENDING ON THE CONSTANT.

53

IF I UNDERSTOOD ONLY ONE THING,
I WOULD WANT TO USE IT TO FOLLOW THE TAO.
MY ONLY FEAR WOULD BE ONE OF PRIDE.
THE TAO GOES IN THE LEVEL PLACES,
BUT PEOPLE PREFER TO TAKE THE SHORT CUTS.
IF TOO MUCH TIME IS SPENT CLEANING THE HOUSE
THE LAND WILL BECOME NEGLECTED AND FULL OF WEEDS,
AND THE GRANARIES WILL SOON BECOME EMPTY
BECAUSE THERE IS NO ONE OUT WORKING THE FIELDS.
TO WEAR FANCY CLOTHES AND ORNAMENTS,
TO HAVE YOUR FILL OF FOOD AND DRINK
AND TO WASTE ALL OF YOUR MONEY BUYING POSSESSIONS
IS CALLED THE CRIME OF EXCESS.
OH, HOW THESE THINGS GO AGAINST THE WAY OF THE TAO!

THAT WHICH IS WELL BUILT
WILL NEVER BE TORN DOWN.
THAT WHICH IS WELL LATCHED
CANNOT SLIP AWAY.
THOSE WHO DO THINGS WELL
WILL BE HONORED FROM GENERATION TO GENERATION.

IF THIS IDEA IS CULTIVATED IN THE INDIVIDUAL,
THEN HIS VIRTUE WILL BECOME GENUINE.
IF THIS IDEA IS CULTIVATED IN YOUR FAMILY,
THEN VIRTUE IN YOUR FAMILY WILL BE GREAT.
IF THIS IDEA IS CULTIVATED IN YOUR COMMUNITY,
THEN VIRTUE WILL GO A LONG WAY.
IF THIS IDEA IS CULTIVATED IN YOUR COUNTRY,
THEN VIRTUE WILL BE IN MANY PLACES.
IF THIS IDEA IS CULTIVATED IN THE WORLD,
THEN VIRTUE WILL BE WITH EVERYONE.

THEN OBSERVE THE PERSON FOR WHAT THE PERSON DOES,
AND OBSERVE THE FAMILY FOR WHAT IT DOES,
AND OBSERVE THE COMMUNITY FOR WHAT IT DOES,
AND OBSERVE THE COUNTRY FOR WHAT IT DOES,
AND OBSERVE THE WORLD FOR WHAT IT DOES.
HOW DO I KNOW THIS SAYING IS TRUE?
I OBSERVE THESE THINGS AND SEE.

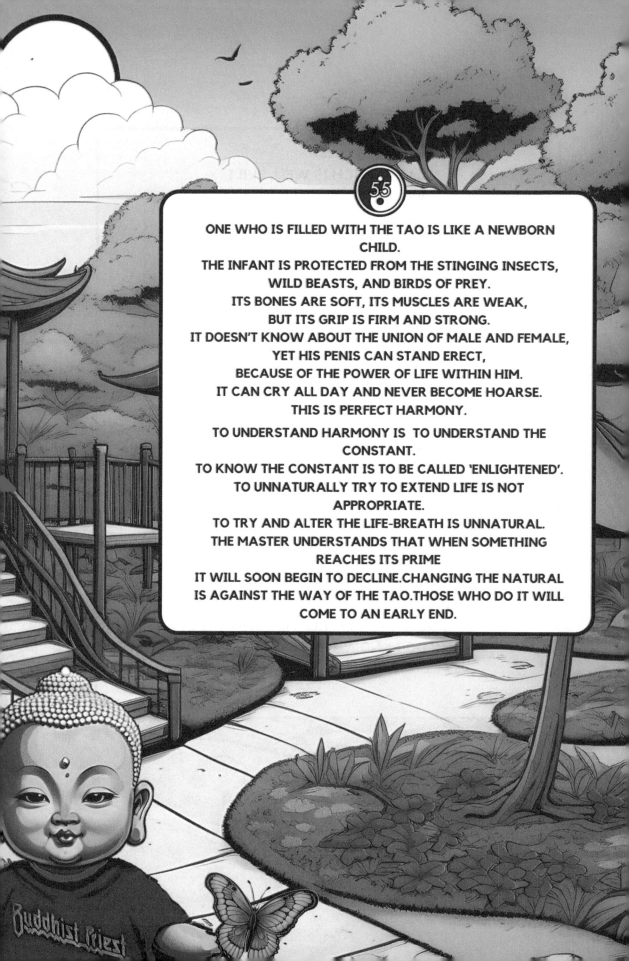

55

ONE WHO IS FILLED WITH THE TAO IS LIKE A NEWBORN CHILD.
THE INFANT IS PROTECTED FROM THE STINGING INSECTS, WILD BEASTS, AND BIRDS OF PREY.
ITS BONES ARE SOFT, ITS MUSCLES ARE WEAK, BUT ITS GRIP IS FIRM AND STRONG.
IT DOESN'T KNOW ABOUT THE UNION OF MALE AND FEMALE, YET HIS PENIS CAN STAND ERECT, BECAUSE OF THE POWER OF LIFE WITHIN HIM.
IT CAN CRY ALL DAY AND NEVER BECOME HOARSE.
THIS IS PERFECT HARMONY.

TO UNDERSTAND HARMONY IS TO UNDERSTAND THE CONSTANT.
TO KNOW THE CONSTANT IS TO BE CALLED 'ENLIGHTENED'.
TO UNNATURALLY TRY TO EXTEND LIFE IS NOT APPROPRIATE.
TO TRY AND ALTER THE LIFE-BREATH IS UNNATURAL.
THE MASTER UNDERSTANDS THAT WHEN SOMETHING REACHES ITS PRIME
IT WILL SOON BEGIN TO DECLINE.CHANGING THE NATURAL IS AGAINST THE WAY OF THE TAO.THOSE WHO DO IT WILL COME TO AN EARLY END.

56

THOSE WHO KNOW DO NOT TALK.
THOSE WHO TALK DO NOT KNOW.

STOP TALKING, MEDITATE IN SILENCE,
BLUNT YOUR SHARPNESS, RELEASE YOUR WORRIES,
HARMONIZE YOUR INNER LIGHT,
AND BECOME ONE WITH THE DUST.
DOING THIS IS THE CALLED THE
DARK AND MYSTERIOUS IDENTITY.

THOSE WHO HAVE ACHIEVED
THE MYSTERIOUS IDENTITY
CANNOT BE APPROACHED, AND
THEY CANNOT BE ALIENATED.
THEY CANNOT BE BENEFITED
NOR HARMED.
THEY CANNOT BE MADE NOBLE
NOR TO SUFFER DISGRACE.
THIS MAKES THEM THE MOST
NOBLE OF ALL UNDER THE HEAVENS.

GOVERN YOUR COUNTRY WITH INTEGRITY,
WEAPONS OF WAR CAN BE USED WITH GREAT CUNNING,
BUT LOYALTY IS ONLY WON BY NOT-DOING.
HOW DO I KNOW THE WAY THINGS ARE?
BY THESE:

THE MORE PROHIBITIONS YOU MAKE,
THE POORER PEOPLE WILL BE.
THE MORE WEAPONS YOU POSSES,
THE GREATER THE CHAOS IN YOUR COUNTRY.
THE MORE KNOWLEDGE THAT IS ACQUIRED,
THE STRANGER THE WORLD WILL BECOME.
THE MORE LAWS THAT YOU MAKE,
THE GREATER THE NUMBER OF CRIMINALS.

THEREFORE THE MASTER SAYS: I DO NOTHING,
AND PEOPLE BECOME GOOD BY THEMSELVES. I SEEK PEACE,
AND PEOPLE TAKE CARE OF THEIR OWN PROBLEMS.
I DO NOT MEDDLE IN THEIR PERSONAL LIVES,
AND THE PEOPLE BECOME PROSPEROUS.
I LET GO OF ALL MY DESIRES,AND THE PEOPLE RETURN
TO THE UNCARVED BLOCK.

58

IF A GOVERNMENT IS UNOBTRUSIVE,
THE PEOPLE BECOME WHOLE.
IF A GOVERNMENT IS REPRESSIVE,
THE PEOPLE BECOME TREACHEROUS.

GOOD FORTUNE HAS ITS ROOTS IN DISASTER,
AND DISASTER LURKS WITH GOOD FORTUNE.
WHO KNOWS WHY THESE THINGS HAPPEN,
OR WHEN THIS CYCLE WILL END?
GOOD THINGS SEEM TO CHANGE INTO BAD,
AND BAD THINGS OFTEN TURN OUT FOR GOOD.
THESE THINGS HAVE ALWAYS BEEN HARD TO
COMPREHEND.

THUS THE MASTER MAKES THINGS CHANGE
WITHOUT INTERFERING.
SHE IS PROBING YET CAUSES NO HARM.
STRAIGHTFORWARD, YET DOES NOT IMPOSE HER WILL.
RADIANT, AND EASY ON THE EYE.

THERE IS NOTHING BETTER THAN MODERATION
FOR TEACHING PEOPLE OR SERVING HEAVEN.
THOSE WHO USE MODERATION
ARE ALREADY ON THE PATH TO THE TAO.

THOSE WHO FOLLOW THE TAO EARLY
WILL HAVE AN ABUNDANCE OF VIRTUE.
WHEN THERE IS AN ABUNDANCE OF VIRTUE,
THERE IS NOTHING THAT CANNOT BE DONE.
WHERE THERE IS LIMITLESS ABILITY,
THEN THE KINGDOM IS WITHING YOUR GRASP.
WHEN YOU KNOW THE MOTHER OF THE KINGDOM,
THEN YOU WILL BE LONG ENDURING.

THIS IS SPOKEN OF AS THE DEEP
ROOT AND THE FIRM TRUNK,
THE WAY TO A LONG LIFE AND
GREAT SPIRITUAL VISION.

GOVERNING A LARGE COUNTRY
IS LIKE FRYING SMALL FISH.
TOO MUCH POKING SPOILS THE MEAT.

WHEN THE TAO IS USED TO GOVERN THE WORLD
THEN EVIL WILL LOOSE ITS POWER TO HARM THE PEOPLE.
NOT THAT EVIL WILL NO LONGER EXIST,
BUT ONLY BECAUSE IT HAS LOST ITS POWER.
JUST AS EVIL CAN LOOSE ITS ABILITY TO HARM,
THE MASTER SHUNS THE USE OF VIOLENCE.

IF YOU GIVE EVIL NOTHING TO OPPOSE,
THEN VIRTUE WILL RETURN BY ITSELF.

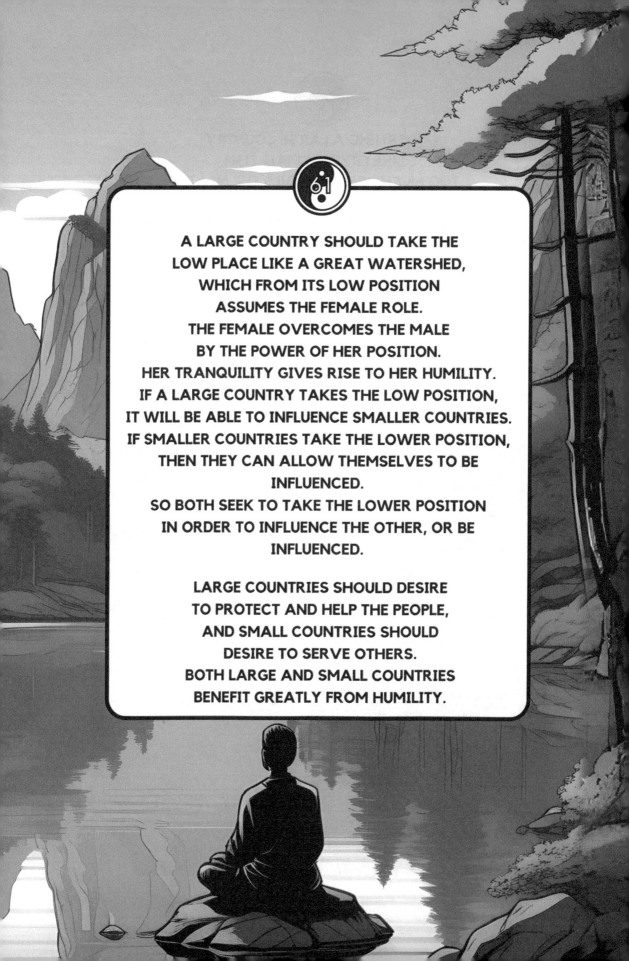

A LARGE COUNTRY SHOULD TAKE THE
LOW PLACE LIKE A GREAT WATERSHED,
WHICH FROM ITS LOW POSITION
ASSUMES THE FEMALE ROLE.
THE FEMALE OVERCOMES THE MALE
BY THE POWER OF HER POSITION.
HER TRANQUILITY GIVES RISE TO HER HUMILITY.
IF A LARGE COUNTRY TAKES THE LOW POSITION,
IT WILL BE ABLE TO INFLUENCE SMALLER COUNTRIES.
IF SMALLER COUNTRIES TAKE THE LOWER POSITION,
THEN THEY CAN ALLOW THEMSELVES TO BE
INFLUENCED.
SO BOTH SEEK TO TAKE THE LOWER POSITION
IN ORDER TO INFLUENCE THE OTHER, OR BE
INFLUENCED.

LARGE COUNTRIES SHOULD DESIRE
TO PROTECT AND HELP THE PEOPLE,
AND SMALL COUNTRIES SHOULD
DESIRE TO SERVE OTHERS.
BOTH LARGE AND SMALL COUNTRIES
BENEFIT GREATLY FROM HUMILITY.

62

THE TAO IS THE TABERNACLE OF CREATION;
IT IS A TREASURE FOR THOSE WHO ARE GOOD,
AND A PLACE OF REFUGE FOR THOSE WHO ARE NOT.

HOW CAN THOSE WHO ARE NOT GOOD BE
ABANDONED?
WORDS THAT ARE BEAUTIFUL ARE WORTH MUCH,
BUT GOOD BEHAVIOR CAN ONLY BE LEARNED BY
EXAMPLE.

WHEN A NEW LEADER TAKES OFFICE,
DON'T GIVE HIM GIFTS AND OFFERINGS.
THESE THINGS ARE NOT AS VALUABLE
AS TEACHING HIM ABOUT THE TAO.

WHY WAS THE TAO ESTEEMED
BY THE ANCIENT MASTERS?
IS IT NOT SAID:
"WITH IT WE FIND WITHOUT LOOKING.
WITH IT WE FIND FORGIVENESS
FOR OUR TRANSGRESSIONS."
THAT IS WHY THE WORLD
CANNOT UNDER STAND IT.

ACT BY NOT ACTING;
DO BY NOT DOING.
ENJOY THE PLAIN AND SIMPLE.
FIND THAT GREATNESS IN THE SMALL.
TAKE CARE OF DIFFICULT PROBLEMS
WHILE THEY ARE STILL EASY;
DO EASY THINGS BEFORE THEY BECOME TOO HARD.

DIFFICULT PROBLEMS ARE BEST SOLVED WHILE THEY
ARE EASY.
GREAT PROJECTS ARE BEST STARTED WHILE THEY
ARE SMALL.
THE MASTER NEVER TAKES ON MORE THAN SHE CAN
HANDLE,
WHICH MEANS THAT SHE LEAVES NOTHING UNDONE.

WHEN AN AFFIRMATION IS GIVEN TOO LIGHTLY,
KEEP YOUR EYES OPEN FOR TROUBLE AHEAD.
WHEN SOMETHING SEEMS TOO EASY,
DIFFICULTY IS HIDING IN THE DETAILS.
THE MASTER EXPECTS GREAT DIFFICULTY,
SO THE TASK IS ALWAYS EASIER THAN PLANNED.

THINGS ARE EASIER TO CONTROL WHILE
THINGS ARE QUIET.
THINGS ARE EASIER TO PLAN FAR IN
ADVANCE.
THINGS BREAK EASIER WHILE THEY ARE STILL
BRITTLE.
THINGS ARE EASIER HID WHILE THEY ARE
STILL SMALL.
PREVENT PROBLEMS BEFORE THEY ARISE.
TAKE ACTION BEFORE THINGS GET OUT OF
HAND.
THE TALLEST TREE BEGINS AS A TINY SPROUT.
THE TALLEST BUILDING STARTS WITH ONE
SHOVEL OF DIRT.
A JOURNEY OF A THOUSAND MILES
STARTS WITH A SINGLE FOOT STEP.

IF YOU RUSH INTO ACTION,
YOU WILL FAIL.
IF YOU HOLD ON TOO TIGHT, YOU WILL LOOSE
YOUR GRIP.
THEREFORE THE MASTER LETS THINGS TAKE
THEIR COURSE
AND THUS NEVER FAILS.
SHE DOESN'T HOLD ON TO THINGS
AND NEVER LOOSES THEM.
BY PURSING YOUR GOALS TOO RELENTLESSLY,
YOU LET THEM SLIP AWAY.
IF YOU ARE AS CONCERNED ABOUT THE
OUTCOME
AS YOU ARE ABOUT THE BEGINNING,
THEN IT IS HARD TO DO
THINGS WRONG.
THE MASTER SEEKS NO POSSESSIONS.
SHE LEARNS BY UNLEARNING,
THUS SHE IS ABLE TO UNDERSTAND ALL
THINGS.
THIS GIVES HER THE ABILITY TO HELP ALL OF
CREATION.

THE ANCIENT MASTERS
WHO UNDERSTOOD THE WAY OF THE TAO,
DID NOT EDUCATE PEOPLE, BUT MADE THEM FORGET.

SMART PEOPLE ARE DIFFICULT TO GUIDE,
BECAUSE THEY THINK THEY ARE TOO CLEVER.
TO USE CLEVERNESS TO RULE A COUNTRY,
IS TO LEAD THE COUNTRY TO RUIN.
TO AVOID CLEVERNESS IN RULING A COUNTRY,
IS TO LEAD THE COUNTRY TO PROSPERITY.

KNOWING THE TWO ALTERNATIVES IS A PATTERN.
REMAINING AWARE OF THE PATTERN IS A VIRTUE.
THIS DARK AND MYSTERIOUS VIRTUE IS PROFOUND.
IT IS OPPOSITE OUR NATURAL INCLINATION,
BUT LEADS TO HARMONY WITH THE HEAVENS.

RIVERS AND SEAS ARE RULERS
OF THE STREAMS OF HUNDREDS OF VALLEYS
BECAUSE OF THE POWER
OF THEIR LOW POSITION.

IF YOU WANT TO BE THE RULER OF PEOPLE,
YOU MUST SPEAK TO THEM LIKE
YOU ARE THEIR SERVANT.
IF YOU WANT TO LEAD OTHER PEOPLE,
YOU MUST PUT THEIR INTEREST
AHEAD OF YOUR OWN.

THE PEOPLE WILL NOT FEEL BURDENED,
IF A WISE PERSON IS IN A POSITION OF POWER.
THE PEOPLE WILL NOT FEEL LIKE
THEY ARE BEING MANIPULATED,
IF A WISE PERSON IS IN FRONT AS THEIR LEADER.
THE WHOLE WORLD WILL ASK FOR HER GUIDANCE,
AND WILL NEVER GET TIRED OF HER.
BECAUSE SHE DOES NOT LIKE TO COMPETE,
NO ONE CAN COMPETE WITH
THE THINGS SHE ACCOMPLISHES.

THE WORLD TALKS ABOUT HONORING THE TAO,
BUT YOU CAN'T TELL IT FROM THEIR ACTIONS.
BECAUSE IT IS THOUGHT OF AS GREAT,
THE WORLD MAKES LIGHT OF IT.
IT SEEMS TOO EASY FOR ANYONE TO USE.

THERE ARE THREE JEWELS THAT I CHERISH:
COMPASSION, MODERATION, AND HUMILITY.WITH COMPASSION,
YOU WILL BE ABLE TO BE BRAVE,WITH MODERATION,
YOU WILL BE ABLE TO GIVE TO OTHERS,WITH HUMILITY,
YOU WILL BE ABLE TO BECOME A GREAT LEADER.

TO ABANDON COMPASSION WHILE SEEKING TO BE BRAVE,
OR ABANDONING MODERATION WHILE BEING BENEVOLENT,
OR ABANDONING HUMILITY WHILE SEEKING TO LEAD
WILL ONLY LEAD TO GREATER TROUBLE.
THE COMPASSIONATE WARRIOR
WILL BE THE WINNER,AND IF COMPASSION IS YOUR
DEFENSE YOU WILL BE SECURE.COMPASSION IS THE PROTECTOR
OF HEAVENS SALVATION.

THE BEST WARRIORS
DO NOT USE VIOLENCE.
THE BEST GENERALS
DO NOT DESTROY
INDISCRIMINATELY.
THE BEST TACTICIANS
TRY TO AVOID CONFRONTATION.
THE BEST LEADERS
BECOMES SERVANTS OF THEIR
PEOPLE.

THIS IS CALLED THE
VIRTUE OF NON-COMPETITION.
THIS IS CALLED THE
POWER TO MANAGE OTHERS.
THIS IS CALLED ATTAINING
HARMONY WITH THE HEAVENS.

THERE IS AN OLD SAYING:
"IT IS BETTER TO BECOME THE PASSIVE
IN ORDER TO SEE WHAT WILL HAPPEN.
IT IS BETTER TO RETREAT A FOOT
THAN TO ADVANCE ONLY AN INCH."

THIS IS CALLED
BEING FLEXIBLE WHILE ADVANCING,
PUSHING BACK WITHOUT USING FORCE,
AND DESTROYING THE ENEMY WITHOUT ENGAGING HIM.
THERE IS NO GREATER DISASTER
THAN UNDERESTIMATING YOUR ENEMY.
UNDERESTIMATING YOUR ENEMY
MEANS LOSING YOUR GREATEST ASSETS.
WHEN EQUAL FORCES MEET IN BATTLE,
VICTORY WILL GO TO THE ONE
THAT ENTERS WITH THE GREATEST SORROW.

MY WORDS ARE EASY TO UNDERSTAND
AND EASIER TO PUT INTO PRACTICE.
YET NO ONE IN THE WORLD
SEEM TO UNDERSTAND THEM,
AND ARE NOT ABLE TO
APPLY WHAT I TEACH.

MY TEACHINGS COME
FROM THE ANCIENTS,
THE THINGS I DO
ARE DONE FOR A REASON.

BECAUSE YOU DO NOT KNOW ME,
YOU ARE NOT ABLE TO
UNDERSTAND MY TEACHINGS.
BECAUSE THOSE WHO
KNOW ME ARE FEW,
MY TEACHINGS BECOME
EVEN MORE PRECIOUS.

KNOWING YOU DON'T
KNOW IS WHOLENESS.
THINKING YOU
KNOW IS A DISEASE.
ONLY BY RECOGNIZING
THAT YOU HAVE AN ILLNESS
CAN YOU MOVE
TO SEEK A CURE.

THE MASTER IS
WHOLE BECAUSE
SHE SEES HER ILLNESSES
AND TREATS THEM,
AND THUS IS ABLE TO
REMAIN WHOLE.

WHEN PEOPLE BECOME
OVERLY BOLD,
THEN DISASTER WILL
SOON ARRIVE.

DO NOT MEDDLE WITH
PEOPLES LIVELIHOOD;
BY RESPECTING THEM THEY
WILL IN TURN RESPECT YOU.
THEREFORE, THE MASTER KNOWS
HERSELF BUT IS NOT ARROGANT.
SHE LOVES HERSELF
BUT ALSO LOVES OTHERS.
THIS IS HOW SHE IS ABLE TO
MAKE APPROPRIATE CHOICES.

BEING OVER BOLD AND CONFIDANT IS DEADLY.
THE WISE USE OF CAUTION WILL KEEP YOU ALIVE.

ONE IS THE WAY TO DEATH,
AND THE OTHER IS THE WAY TO PRESERVE YOUR LIFE.
WHO CAN UNDERSTAND THE WORKINGS OF HEAVEN?

THE TAO OF THE UNIVERSE
DOES NOT COMPETE, YET WINS;
DOES NOT SPEAK, YET RESPONDS;
DOES NOT COMMAND, YET IS OBEYED;
AND DOES ACT, BUT IS GOOD AT DIRECTING.

THE NETS OF HEAVEN ARE WIDE,
BUT NOTHING ESCAPES ITS GRASP.

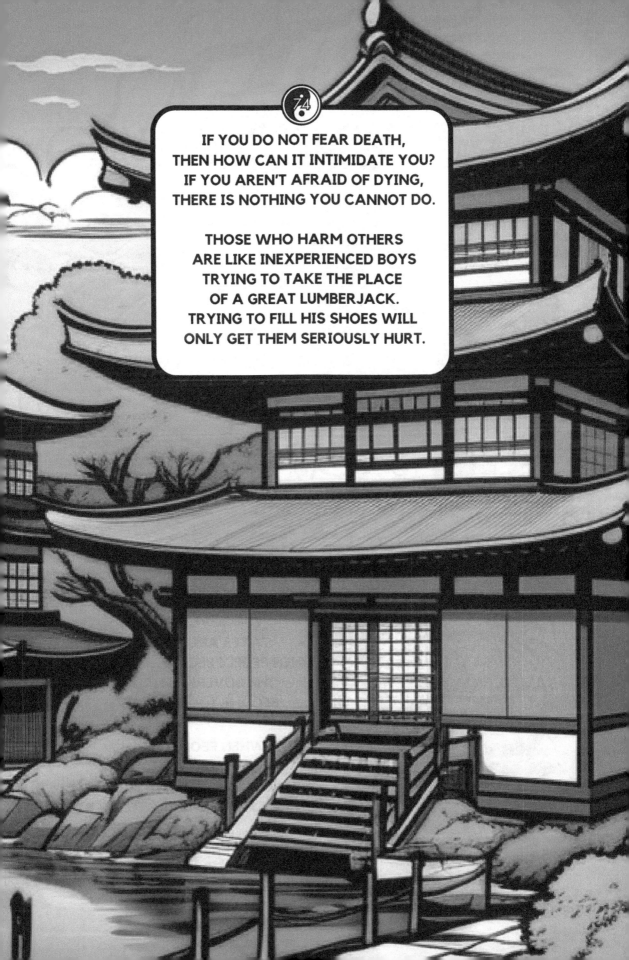

74

IF YOU DO NOT FEAR DEATH,
THEN HOW CAN IT INTIMIDATE YOU?
IF YOU AREN'T AFRAID OF DYING,
THERE IS NOTHING YOU CANNOT DO.

THOSE WHO HARM OTHERS
ARE LIKE INEXPERIENCED BOYS
TRYING TO TAKE THE PLACE
OF A GREAT LUMBERJACK.
TRYING TO FILL HIS SHOES WILL
ONLY GET THEM SERIOUSLY HURT.

WHEN PEOPLE GO HUNGRY,
THE GOVERNMENTS
TAXES ARE TOO HIGH.
WHEN PEOPLE BECOME REBELLIOUS,
THE GOVERNMENT HAS
BECOME TOO INTRUSIVE.

WHEN PEOPLE BEGIN
TO VIEW DEATH LIGHTLY,
WEALTHY PEOPLE HAVE TOO MUCH
WHICH CAUSES OTHERS TO STARVE.

ONLY THOSE WHO DO NOT
CLING TO THEIR LIFE CAN SAVE IT.

THE LIVING ARE SOFT AND YIELDING;
THE DEAD ARE RIGID AND STIFF.
LIVING PLANTS ARE FLEXIBLE AND TENDER;
THE DEAD ARE BRITTLE AND DRY.

THOSE WHO ARE STIFF AND RIGID
ARE THE DISCIPLES OF DEATH.
THOSE WHO ARE SOFT AND YIELDING
ARE THE DISCIPLES OF LIFE.

THE RIGID AND STIFF WILL BE BROKEN.
THE SOFT AND YIELDING WILL OVERCOME.

THE TAO OF HEAVEN
WORKS IN THE WORLD
LIKE THE DRAWING OF A BOW.
THE TOP IS BENT DOWNWARD;
THE BOTTOM IS BENT UP.
THE EXCESS IS TAKEN FROM,
AND THE DEFICIENT IS GIVEN TO.

THE TAO WORKS TO USE THE EXCESS,
AND GIVES TO THAT
WHICH IS DEPLETED.
THE WAY OF PEOPLE IS TO
TAKE FROM THE DEPLETED,
AND GIVE TO THOSE WHO
ALREADY HAVE AN EXCESS.

WHO IS ABLE TO GIVE TO THE
NEEDY FROM THEIR EXCESS?
ONLY SOMEONE WHO IS
FOLLOWING THE WAY OF THE TAO.

THIS IS WHY THE MASTER GIVES
EXPECTING NOTHING IN RETURN.
SHE DOES NOT DWELL ON HER
PAST ACCOMPLISHMENTS,
AND DOES NOT GLORY IN ANY PRAISE.

WATER IS THE SOFTEST AND
MOST YIELDING SUBSTANCE.
YET NOTHING IS
BETTER THAN WATER FOR OVERCOMING
THE HARD AND RIGID,
BECAUSE NOTHING CAN COMPETE WITH IT.

EVERYONE KNOWS THAT
THE SOFT AND YIELDING
OVERCOMES THE RIGID AND HARD,
BUT FEW CAN PUT THIS
KNOWLEDGE INTO PRACTICE.

THEREFORE THE MASTER SAYS:
"ONLY HE WHO IS THE LOWEST
SERVANT OF THE KINGDOM,
IS WORTHY TO BECOME ITS RULER.
HE WHO IS WILLING TACKLE THE
MOST UNPLEASANT TASKS,
IS THE BEST RULER IN THE WORLD."

DIFFICULTIES REMAIN,
EVEN AFTER SOLVING A PROBLEM.
HOW THEN CAN WE CONSIDER THAT AS GOOD?

THEREFORE THE MASTER
DOES WHAT SHE KNOWS IS RIGHT,
AND MAKES NO DEMANDS OF OTHERS.
A VIRTUOUS PERSON WILL DO THE RIGHT THING,
AND PERSONS WITH NO VIRTUE
WILL TAKE ADVANTAGE OF OTHERS.

THE TAO DOES NOT CHOOSE SIDES;
THE GOOD PERSON RECEIVES FROM THE TAO
BECAUSE SHE IS ON ITS SIDE.

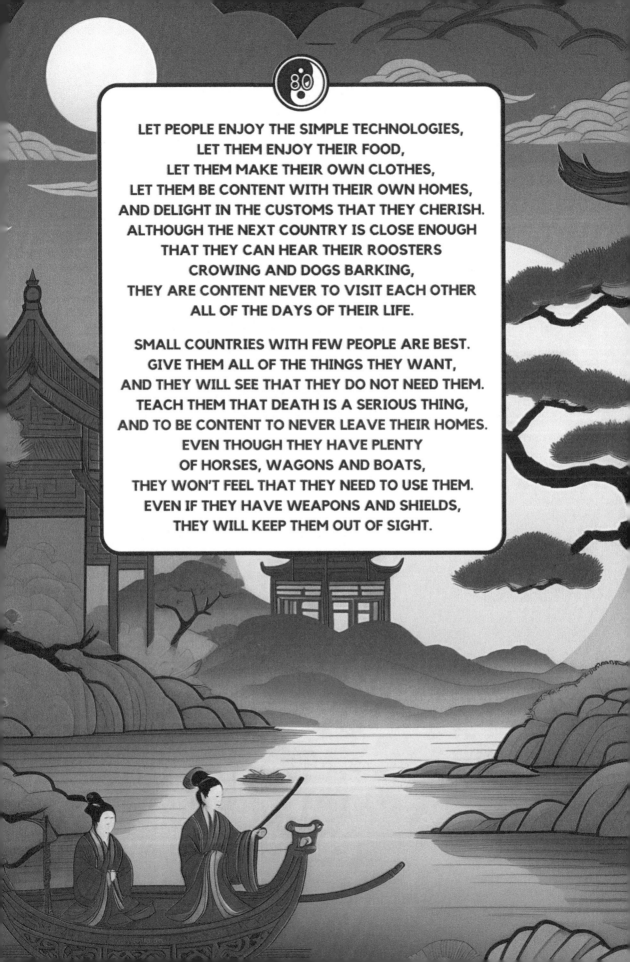

LET PEOPLE ENJOY THE SIMPLE TECHNOLOGIES,
LET THEM ENJOY THEIR FOOD,
LET THEM MAKE THEIR OWN CLOTHES,
LET THEM BE CONTENT WITH THEIR OWN HOMES,
AND DELIGHT IN THE CUSTOMS THAT THEY CHERISH.
ALTHOUGH THE NEXT COUNTRY IS CLOSE ENOUGH
THAT THEY CAN HEAR THEIR ROOSTERS
CROWING AND DOGS BARKING,
THEY ARE CONTENT NEVER TO VISIT EACH OTHER
ALL OF THE DAYS OF THEIR LIFE.

SMALL COUNTRIES WITH FEW PEOPLE ARE BEST.
GIVE THEM ALL OF THE THINGS THEY WANT,
AND THEY WILL SEE THAT THEY DO NOT NEED THEM.
TEACH THEM THAT DEATH IS A SERIOUS THING,
AND TO BE CONTENT TO NEVER LEAVE THEIR HOMES.
EVEN THOUGH THEY HAVE PLENTY
OF HORSES, WAGONS AND BOATS,
THEY WON'T FEEL THAT THEY NEED TO USE THEM.
EVEN IF THEY HAVE WEAPONS AND SHIELDS,
THEY WILL KEEP THEM OUT OF SIGHT.

TRUE WORDS DO NOT SOUND BEAUTIFUL;
BEAUTIFUL SOUNDING WORDS ARE NOT TRUE.
WISE MEN DON'T NEED TO DEBATE;
MEN WHO NEED TO DEBATE ARE NOT WISE.
WISE MEN ARE NOT SCHOLARS,
AND SCHOLARS ARE NOT WISE.
THE MASTER DESIRES NO POSSESSIONS.
SINCE THE THINGS SHE DOES ARE FOR THE PEOPLE,
SHE HAS MORE THAN SHE NEEDS.
THE MORE SHE GIVES TO OTHERS,
THE MORE SHE HAS FOR HERSELF.

THE TAO OF HEAVEN NOURISHES BY NOT FORCING.
THE TAO OF THE WISE PERSON ACTS BY NOT COMPETING.

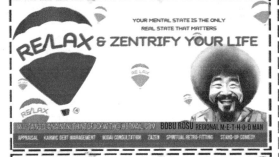

Made in United States
Orlando, FL
16 January 2025

57343112R00076